FOREWORD BY JIMMY EVANS

*The Story of How
God Transformed My Life & Marriage
from Brokenness to Blessing*

# FROM PAIN TO PARADISE

KAREN EVANS

Copyright © 2020 by XO Publishing.

This book, or parts thereof, may not be reproduced in any form or by any means without written permission from the publisher, except brief passages for purposes of reviews. For information, address MarriageToday™.

P.O. Box 59888 Dallas, Texas 75229
1-800-380-6330
or visit our website at marriagetoday.com

XO Publishing

ISBN 978-0-9600831-2-1

All Scripture quotations, unless otherwise indicated, are taken from the Holy Bible, New King James Version®, NKJV®. Copyright © 1982 by Thomas Nelson. Used by permission of Zondervan. All rights reserved.

Scripture quotations marked (NIV) are from the Holy Bible, New InternationalVersion®, NIV®. Copyright ©1973, 1978, 1984, 2011 by Biblica, Inc.™ Used by permission of Zondervan.
All rights reserved

Scripture quotations marked (KJV) King James Version, Authorized King James Version, Public Domain.

All rights reserved. No portion of this publication may be reproduced, stored in a retrieval system, or transmitted in any form by any means—electronic, mechanical, photocopying, recording, or any other—without prior permission from the publisher.

XO Publishing has no responsibility for the persistence or accuracy or URLs for external or third-party Internet websites referred to in this publication and does not guarantee that any content on such websites is, or will remain, accurate or appropriate.

Printed in the United States of America.

To Jesus,
Your love and words healed and redeemed my life.
I am not the same person because of You.

**Psalm 30:5**

*"Weeping may last for the night, but joy comes in the morning."*

# CONTENTS

Foreword by Jimmy Evans. . . . . . . . . . . . . . . . . . . . . . . .11

Acknowledgments. . . . . . . . . . . . . . . . . . . . . . . . . . . . . 15

*Chapter 1* . . . . . . . . . . . . . . . . . . . . . . . . . . . . . . . . . . 19
Life in the Spotlight

*Chapter 2* . . . . . . . . . . . . . . . . . . . . . . . . . . . . . . . . . . 33
Two Wounded Hearts

*Chapter 3* . . . . . . . . . . . . . . . . . . . . . . . . . . . . . . . . . . 47
A Fractured Foundation

*Chapter 4* . . . . . . . . . . . . . . . . . . . . . . . . . . . . . . . . . . 61
Spontaneous Combustion

*Chapter 5* . . . . . . . . . . . . . . . . . . . . . . . . . . . . . . . . . . 75
The Search for Answers

*Chapter 6* . . . . . . . . . . . . . . . . . . . . . . . . . . . . . . . . . 89
The Power of Prayer

*Chapter 7* . . . . . . . . . . . . . . . . . . . . . . . . . . . . . . . . .101
Toxic Thoughts and Wrong Words

*Chapter 8* . . . . . . . . . . . . . . . . . . . . . . . . . . . . . . . . .113
A Woman and a Well

*Chapter 9* . . . . . . . . . . . . . . . . . . . . . . . . . . . . . . . . 125
The Perfect Storm

*Chapter 10* . . . . . . . . . . . . . . . . . . . . . . . . . . . . . . . .137
A Time to Change

# FOREWORD

For many years Karen and I have conducted marriage seminars all over the world. Because Karen doesn't teach, I am the one who shares the story of how God saved our marriage from the brink of divorce. But there is a big difference between the way I tell the story and how Karen tells it. As I read this book I was astounded at the details Karen remembered about how we dated and the early years of our marriage. When I share the story I tell the big picture. But in this book Karen shares the step-by-step and blow-by-blow of how we went from two young people madly in love to a young married couple on the brink of divorce, to a healthy married couple deeply in love again.

This book carefully chronicles the lives of two very dysfunctional people and how the power of God intervened to save us from disaster. We were both damaged goods when we got married and it is only by God's grace that we made it. But the good news is that we did make it and our message is that you can make it too. The same love and grace that God extended to us He will extend to anyone who calls upon Him for help. The secret of our lives and marriage is putting God first. When Karen and I met I was not a believer. I got saved a week before we married and as you will read in this book – it wasn't under good conditions. But Karen always had a heart for God. All through our dating relationship she sought God. But I didn't understand at the time the depth of pain she was experiencing on a personal level. All I knew was that she was beautiful, fun to be with and extremely shy. But as our relationship developed the worst in me came out. And it just made the pain in Karen's life worse. In the midst of all of it I didn't want to lose her but I didn't know how to keep her.

We were both so wounded and dysfunctional. Even after becoming a believer I was still chauvinistic, domineering and verbally abusive. Without a doubt I would have destroyed our marriage if it had not been for Karen's pursuit of God. I was a very selfish and insensitive man who was redeemed by a godly woman. And what is even more remarkable is the fact that she redeemed me through her love as she was going through incredible pain in her own life. A lot of her pain was in her the day I met her. But a lot of it came from me too.

If I have ever met a person who is an expert in dealing with inner pain it is Karen. She is the strongest person I know. But it isn't a strength she was born with. It is a strength that has been forged in the fires of life and marriage as she clung to God and wouldn't let go. That is what this book is about. It is about Karen's story of how she faced every storm of life and came out more in love with God. It is about a woman who has endured incredible inner pain and found true healing in the arms of God. It is about a godly wife who overcame the pain of a distracted and abusive husband by the power and love of God.

I am so proud of Karen for writing this book. This is the true story of her life and our marriage. And the most important character in this story is God.

Jimmy Evans
*Co-host of MarriageToday*

# ACKNOWLEDGMENTS

There is no doubt that this book was written because of the Lord's unfailing love and kindness towards me even when I barely knew who He was. He took His precious Words and literally healed and changed me. I am daily reminded of how much He has done for me so I can live my life freed by His Truth. The more I read the Bible the more I'm amazed by His grace and love.

Also, my husband Jimmy who continued to fight for our marriage and never stopped believing in who I was created to be. We truly were meant to be together and I'm so grateful he didn't give up.

To my parents who instilled moral values and hard work you both have given me so much.

To my children, Julie and Brent thank you for continuing our values and God's in yourselves and our precious grandchildren, Elle, Abby, Kate, Reed, and Luke. Your own families are a testimony of what the Lord has done.

Thank you to Shelly for all of your support and assistance. We could not do what we do without you.

When I look back on all the pain and trials I went through, the beauty of who the Lord and all my family are to me, it was worth it all.

# CHAPTER ONE

*Life in the Spotlight*

# 01

## *Life in the Spotlight*

Sitting beside my husband, Jimmy, on the set of our television program, *Marriage Today*, I blinked against the bright lights. Jimmy reached over and grabbed my hand, his touch taking me back to the girl I'd been when we met. Back then if I'd been interrogated for hours under these same lights about how I would live my life, I would never have imagined this.

On the contrary.

In those days, if someone had told me we would wind up hosting a television show, I probably would have bolted like the Old Testament prophet Jonah. I was so shy that just shaking someone's hand and trying to make eye contact turned me into a quivering, blushing mass of insecurities. I would have preferred a slow death in the belly of a whale to bright lights, rolling cameras and viewing audiences.

As if sensing my thoughts, Jimmy glanced at me and smiled. The instant our eyes met, I felt comfort from Jimmy's strength and the love we share and thanked God for the miracle of it. This was why I was here, taping a television program to help people with their marriages—so God could do for others what He's done for us.

"That's a wrap," the director said a few minutes later. The red recording light on the cameras blinked off and the lights dimmed. Making my way off the set, a woman stopped me.

"I want to have a marriage just like yours," she said. "I want to be married to a man like Jimmy."

I hear that a lot. And though I understand why, I must admit, I'm sometimes tempted to chuckle. *Of course!* I think. *Any woman would want to be married to a man like Jimmy is today.*

But he wasn't always like this. Neither was I.

When our relationship began we were completely different. So different that most people find it difficult to picture the less-than-idyllic marital path we've traveled: the years of vicious verbal battles that lay behind us, the countless nights we spent in cold silence, the endless floods of hot tears that just wouldn't stop. Looking at us now, holding hands and talking about Jesus, it's hard for anybody to imagine us as we used to be: Jimmy, angry and accusing, haughty and hateful, treating me more like a slave than the love of his life; me, broken-hearted and aching with self-condemnation, desperately trying to please him one moment, then erupting with destructive, pent-up fury the next.

For what seemed like an eternity, that was our reality.

Which is why I sometimes want to say to those like the precious woman who stopped me on the set that day, "Seriously? You want a marriage like mine? You want to cry yourself to sleep every night—*for years?*"

No. Nobody wants that.

I certainly didn't. But it's what I got. From the beginning, my marriage was marked by the letter P—Pain. While the later years have been paradise, the early years pierced both Jimmy and me with pain at its most primitive level.

He has written books about our experience. He's preached sermons about it and told our stories in conferences. For the most part, however, my side of what happened has remained untold. Although I've answered some questions and shared a little in our conferences and on TV, I haven't fully revealed—at least until now—how I made my journey through the pain to the marriage we enjoy today.

The reason is simple. Unlike my husband, I'm not a teacher or preacher. I'm not an accomplished public speaker. I'm a low-profile person who's most comfortable working quietly behind the scenes. But people keep asking me to tell my story, so in this book, that is what I will try my best to do.

I pray that what I have to say will bless and encourage you. I hope it will remind you of the wonders our patient, all-powerful God can do in the midst of even the most hopeless situations and for even the most messed-up people. But I also want to give you fair warning: I'm not going to sugarcoat my experiences. I won't pretend they were something other than what they were. I'm going to tell my story with stark honesty, as completely as I can.

And I'm going to start at the beginning.

Not with the early days of our train-wreck of a marriage, but with the old familiar story of how a girl met a boy and fell in love. Jimmy and I were just teenagers when that happened to us. We were barely even old enough to have what might be called "a past." Yet it was our past that set the stage for our turbulent relationship. Strange as it seems, even at the tender age of 16 when we first got together, we'd both somehow managed to accumulate a precarious pile of emotional baggage.

And that baggage is where our trouble, and our story, began.

## *Definitely Handsome but Not My Type*

Jimmy first came across my radar in biology class during the second semester of our sophomore year in high school. I sat in the front of the class, he sat at the back. From all appearances we had nothing in common. Naïve and shy, I blushed my way through the class surrounded by friends who delighted in mentioning certain biological terms that turned me into a tomato head (which they found hysterical). Jimmy, from his seat on the back row, played the role of my polar opposite, the always-cool, class clown.

Like most high schools, ours had a social hierarchy system. The boys belonged to one of three main groups: the Athletes, the Hoods and the Nerds. Jimmy ran with the Hoods and looked a lot like James Dean, swaggering with confidence. He had a great body which he showed off by wearing skinny jeans and an amazing shirt.

I assumed he wore that shirt almost every day because he knew how great he looked in it. I would never have guessed it was simply because his parents couldn't afford to buy him very many clothes.

Although Jimmy was handsome, I wasn't really attracted to him at first. I only noticed him because he sometimes hung around with a friend of mine from homeroom. "Hey, do you know Jimmy Evans?" she asked one day.

"Yeah, I see him all the time," I said. "He's always got his arm around some girl."

"Well, he wants to take you out."

*What? He's interested in dating me?* Startled, I pondered the information. I'd only gone out on three or four dates at the time and none of them had been happy experiences. They'd mostly been wrestling matches with me fending off unwanted advances and saying things like, "No, you're not kissing me!" An evening with Jimmy Evans could easily involve more of the same. Not at all my type, he was outgoing, boisterous, and a ladies' man.

I might not have been interested in him at all if not for his eyes. I saw a softness and vulnerability in them. While he came across as a tough guy, I didn't think he was who he portrayed himself to be. I suspected that underneath his tough exterior, he was tender.

## A Dented Car, a First Date, and Three Dog Night

"Okay," I said. "I'll go out with him."

"Cool! He's going to take you to a Three Dog Night concert!" This was back in the 1970s and my friend helped me pick out black pants with a flare at the bottom to wear to the big event. Nervous and excited, I waited for the phone to ring. But days passed and Jimmy didn't call.

I began to wonder if my friend's information had been solid. But, sure enough, it was. On the day of the concert he finally asked me to go.

When he came to pick me up that evening and saw the relative affluence of my neighborhood, he made sure to park his car with the most dented and beat-up side turned away from our house. If he was hoping to impress my parents, he failed. At the door, my dad glowered at him.

My parents had freaked when I'd told them about our date. "Who is this Jimmy?" they'd said. "We don't know anything about him!" Hoping to spare him the third degree, I hurried to get him out of their line of fire.

The concert was great that night. But the thing I enjoyed most was how easy Jimmy was to talk to. His open, honest way of communicating captivated me.

Even as a teenager I had strong boundaries where the truth was concerned. I always believed I could handle anything—no matter how bad—as long as people were honest with me. So I found Jimmy's truthfulness about his lifestyle oddly comforting. As one date led to another, he openly admitted to me that he drank and partied hard with his friends. He even acknowledged he'd been sexually active—at least until he started going out with me.

I don't think he'd ever experienced anyone like me before; I didn't let him kiss me until our seventh date. He knew I was pure and intended to stay that way until I was married. So our deep connection came only through communication. We spent hours on the phone each evening and talked about everything. No topic was off limits.

I'd spent most of my life up to that point too tongue-tied to talk. Yet with Jimmy it seemed I could express everything that had been bottled up in me for years. I'd never been able to talk to anyone like I did with him.

I was smitten.

The kind of emotional trust Jimmy and I shared was intoxicating. We got each other in a way that nobody else in our lives ever had.

Still, if I'd known what was ahead, I would've run for my life. I had no idea how relationally dysfunctional we both were or how unrealistic our expectations. Like most people, we expected the love we felt for each other to heal our wounds and fill the holes in our souls.

But it was never going to happen. Instead, because of the unresolved pain, problems, and imperfect family histories we carried into our relationship, we would wind up hurting each other even more.

## *Hummingbird in an Eagle's Nest*

Please don't misunderstand me. I don't mention our family histories because I think our parents are to blame for our marriage problems. I believe both my parents and Jimmy's did their best for us and I appreciate them deeply. I also believe that we, like everyone else, are responsible for our own choices. But there's no denying that family dynamics can have a definite impact on how we perceive ourselves and the choices we make.

They certainly did in my case.

Born to parents with remarkably strong, dominant personalities, I started my life as a kind of genetic anomaly, with a timid, introverted temperament. While my parents feared nothing, just shaking hands with someone almost threw me into a panic. Talk about an awkward set of family dynamics. It was as though two eagles had somehow given birth to a little hummingbird fluttering with anxiety.

Because I was naturally inclined to look outward for direction and approval, I always thought I needed to be told what to do. And my parents, as very forceful leaders, were quick to oblige. It turned out to be the perfect setup for a toxic relationship.

To further complicate matters, my mother's strength had been forged in the fire of almost unthinkable adversity. As a youngster who always loved being outdoors, at only 14 years old she was visiting her uncle's farm in Michigan for the summer when she'd suffered a terrible accident. Riding on the back of a hay chopper she caught her pant leg in the machinery. Quicker than a lightening bolt in a storm, she lost her left leg and arm.

She remained conscious as her uncle carried her to his pickup and rushed her to the hospital.

My mother, rather than allowing the experience to crush her, used it to develop a fierce independence that propelled her into a successful life. Back then people didn't believe in talking about traumatic events or emotional issues. So rarely did anyone in her family talk about the incident. It was stored away, like musty boxes in the dark recesses of an attic. Even as a young adult my mother never told us what had happened to her. My brother and my sister and I assumed she'd been maimed in a washing machine accident.

"Never open the lid when it's washing!" she always warned us. "If you do you'll lose an arm and leg!" We didn't learn the truth until years later when we pressed her for details.

The up side of how my mother dealt with her trauma was that the lost limbs never defined her. No one who's ever met my mother would call her handicapped. She isn't; never has been. She is a whole person—beautiful, competent and independent.

Still, I can't imagine any child suffering such a trauma without forming a tough emotional barrier to ward off the pain, like a turtle forms a shell to protect its tender belly. That may explain why there wasn't much nurturing in our home. No warm fuzzy expressions of love. There was little tenderness or sympathy when we were sick or injured.

Instead, my mother expressed her concern for us in other ways. She carefully guarded how we spent our time, for instance. Although we owned a TV, she only allowed us to watch it at certain times and for only an hour a day. Determined to keep us from turning into couch potatoes, she sent us outside to play. On long summer days she drove us to the country club to swim and spend time with friends, dropping us off in the morning and picking us up in the afternoon.

As a result, like my mother, I learned to relish being outdoors. To this day I still love it.

## Writing Letters to God

One important thing to note about my family is that none of us were born again. We knew nothing about having a personal relationship with Jesus. My parents did believe in God, however, and they taught my brother and sister and me to do the same.

I remember one night when I was in the second grade, camping out in the backyard, surrounded by the scent of fresh mowed grass and lightning bugs flitting around like Tinker Bell. I looked up at the thousands of stars twinkling like fairy dust in the sky and asked, "Dad, who made the stars?"

"God."

"Who's God?"

There under the night sky, Dad explained that God had created everything. I looked from the sky to the grass, the trees, and the tent—and I was amazed. "God created it all!" I whispered. From then on, I was drawn to Him. I wanted to know Him so badly that I even started writing letters to Him.

My mother fueled my spiritual passion by continuing to point out God's handiwork in nature. When we took vacations she always reminded us that the mountains, the lakes, the sea, and stars were all His spectacular displays.

In spite of this, there wasn't much peace or tranquility in our home. My dad was a mostly absentee father, traveling a great deal on business. That left my mother to handle most of the responsibility for raising us kids—and we definitely were a handful. My brother in particular had emotional issues growing up which presented my parents with perpetual challenges. His problems were the vortex of a whirlwind that whipped through our home. His tongue, like the tail of the tornado, wounded and ripped our whole family.

For years, he told me over and over, "You're fat, ugly and stupid!"

By the time I started eighth grade I believed it. The worst year of my life, the school system opened a new junior high that year and I had to leave my friends behind to attend it. In that strange new environment my insecurities rocketed. Trying to navigate my way around a new school as a total stranger, my brother's words became my own personal revelation. I *am* ugly! I *am* fat! I *really am* stupid!

You may think I just had a very poor self image, and you'd be right. But I have pictures of myself in eighth grade. They bear witness to my homely appearance and the 30 extra pounds I needed to lose. Being overweight in my family wasn't acceptable and most everyone else was thin back then, so I couldn't figure out why I was so chubby. *What is the matter with me?* I wondered.

Now that I'm an adult, I know: I comforted myself with food—and at that stage in my life I needed a *lot* of comfort. I was hurt and angry about what was happening at home. My brother's struggles were draining our entire household. He constantly bullied and attacked my sister and me. Once he'd even stabbed me with a fork.

After I developed breasts, he delighted in doubling his fists and using them as punching bags. But my parents, exhausted from dealing with him, didn't protect me, nor did they punish him.

The injustice of the situation not only drove me to drown my sorrows in the giant cinnamon rolls served in the school cafeteria, it also stoked a rage in me that roared into a ball of fire.

I couldn't get away with talking back to my parents, so when my anger boiled over, I ran to my room, slammed the door and threw shoes. Then I hid in my closet and cried for hours on end. In time, my anger turned inward and I lived in a state of chronic depression. I shut down, never expressing my emotions. I wouldn't talk. I refused to look my family members in the eye. I closed myself in my room and hid in an emotional cave.

Why is this important? Because it became an unhealthy coping mechanism for me; a pattern of behavior which I repeated many times while Jimmy and I were dating and long after we were married.

Worst of all, for decades it cast a cold and forbidding shadow over my relationship with the greatest Love of my life…not Jimmy, but One I wrote letters to as a little girl. The God I desperately needed and was too afraid to trust.

# CHAPTER TWO

*Two Wounded Hearts*

# 02

*Two Wounded Hearts*

By the time I started dating Jimmy, I'd found ways to pull myself together—at least on the outside. My yo-yo dieting had paid off, melting away those unsightly extra 30 pounds. Summer days lying by the pool with my friends had tanned my skin to a deep golden brown and bleached my hair honey blonde. All of a sudden guys were noticing me—in a good way.

Although I was still depressed at home, otherwise things were looking up. Especially when I was with Jimmy, I felt alive! In our early months together, as we spent countless hours just sharing what was on our hearts, our trust for each other continued to deepen. When I told him why I felt sad at home, he supported and validated me and I did the same for him.

Truth be told, Jimmy needed that validation almost as much as I did. Despite his apparent strength and self-sufficiency, he battled his own brand of insecurity. Having grown up in a financially strapped family, he'd often had to go without the luxuries others around him enjoyed. Wearing the same shirt to school almost every day had been the least of his problems. He'd often been hungry because there wasn't enough food at his house.

Like me, Jimmy also knew what it was like to feel alone. His parents worked long hours outside the home, not because they weren't committed to him and his two older brothers, but because they needed the money. Jimmy's father, determined to pull himself and his family out of the poverty he himself had been trapped in as a kid, worked day and night. So did Jimmy's mother. As a result, the three boys spent the majority of their time unsupervised with the oldest left in charge. As in my family, that didn't work out very well.

Jimmy also grew up in a spiritual void. Although his parents dropped him off each Sunday at church and picked him up after service, he hated the entire experience. To him, it was boring to the point of being mind numbing.

In high school, he started visiting a different church with a friend and went with him to the summer camp. He enjoyed that more but it didn't help much. What he learned about the Lord touched his head but not his heart. So his behavior didn't change. He carried on with his wild ways, playing poker and getting drunk with his friends on Friday nights, and going downtown to pick up girls.

Jimmy's friends meant the world to him. And he made it clear when we started dating that, as much as he cherished our relationship, he would not allow it to infringe on his time with them. I understood this and accepted it, but I trusted him to be faithful to me, and he was.

## The Beginning of a Toxic Dance

Things between us were wonderful for a while, but as the newness of our romance wore off we began to have horrible fights. He didn't hit me; there was never physical violence. The blows he struck were only verbal. But they still left their mark.

The old adage that sticks and stones may break my bones but words can never hurt me is a lie. I'd known that long before I met Jimmy. My brother's words had wounded me on the inside for years. They'd left me with emotional scars that, unlike physical bruises that heal and disappear, refused to go away.

Jimmy took up where my brother left off. He turned his words against me, wielding them with such deadly force they should have been registered as lethal weapons. I couldn't even come close to matching his verbal skill. Whenever we argued he hammered me until I was convinced the conflict was entirely my fault. I took the blame for his unhappiness and then he stepped into the role my dominant parents had filled: He started giving me orders. He told me what to do and how I should treat him.

For a while, I simply cowered under his attacks and struggled to adapt. But then one day I snapped. Apparently somewhere in my DNA, mixed in with all my timidity, I'd inherited a stubborn streak—a sliver of my mother's backbone or a tiny cord of my father's strength—and suddenly it kicked in. My anger flared and I decided I'd had enough.

Refusing to take it anymore, I walked out of the relationship. "I'm out of here!" I said.

After we broke up, Jimmy was miserable. He came back to me with a tender, soft attitude, like the guy I always believed him to be, and I gave him another chance. Even back then I realized we each had damaged hearts. That's where we connected—in our wounds.

Once we got back together, the cycle geared up again. Jimmy abused me with his words, I took it as long as I could, and then I broke up with him. As soon as we broke up, something switched in Jimmy and he came back to me, humble, just like before. For a while things were good and then the cycle repeated.

We were in a toxic dance, moving closer to one another, then wounding each other and dancing apart. We each had troubled, dysfunctional relationships at home. Now we'd developed what felt normal to both of us—a troubled, dysfunctional relationship of our own.

## *Desperate Days and Sleepless Nights*

In hindsight I can see that even during those miserable, messed up days, God had His hand on us. So it's no surprise that, just like Jimmy's friend had once invited him to the Baptist Church, one of my friends did the same. I accepted her invitation and for the first time in my life got spiritually fed. It made me so hungry for more of God that I started attending a Bible study at 6:30 in the morning.

Although I didn't know it then, the Lord was also working in my parents' lives. They'd never heard the Gospel message in the church they attended but when I was about sixteen they got involved with the Navigators ministry and ended up getting born again. They continued attending their church and soon all their friends there were getting born again as well.

My parents didn't tell me about any of this, but then I didn't tell them about the spiritual changes taking place in my life either. So nothing at home seemed different. We were all so new at being Christians our behavior hadn't yet changed very much. My mother and father still acted and reacted much like they always had and so did I. As baby believers we didn't have the first clue how to get free from the life-long patterns of thinking that had defined us. Yet, without mentioning it to each other, we were each making tiny incremental steps in a new direction.

Sadly, none of those steps improved the situation with Jimmy. My parents, who had never liked him in the first place, continued to want him out of our lives. My mother went so far as to call her Bible study group and ask them to pray that we would break up.

Their prayers did not avail.

Jimmy and I kept right on fighting, breaking up, and getting back together…fighting, breaking up, and getting back together. And despite my budding Christian faith, it looked like we always would.

Although we fought over all kinds of things, one primary source of tension between us was this: Jimmy didn't want anyone—most especially a woman—telling him what to do. He had a hair trigger about that.

One evening, for instance, we were on the phone and I said, "Jimmy, we need to spend more time together." He reacted as though I'd struck a match to a can of gasoline. He blasted me with such an angry tirade that by the time he finished, I felt ripped to shreds.

After I hung up the phone, I was too upset to sleep. Slipping out of the house in the middle of the night, I walked through the inky darkness to the park. In the back of my mind I thought, *He's going to come looking for me! He'll find me here!*

He didn't, of course.

So I just sat in the park sobbing my heart out and replaying Jimmy's words in my mind. They confirmed everything I'd believed about myself. They confirmed every vile accusation my brother had spewed at me and reminded me that my parents hadn't protected me from my brother's onslaughts for one simple reason—because I wasn't worth protecting.

"God," I prayed, "if this is the way my life is going to be, just let me die! If I have to live in this much pain, just send someone out of that alley to rape and kill me!"

To some, such thoughts might seem shocking. But I'd been so depressed I'd spent years imagining death. I couldn't take my own life because I was afraid to meet God under those circumstances. Yet I believed He approved of what Jimmy said to me. I thought He viewed me much as my brother and my whole family did. To Him, as to them, I was worthless. He most likely wanted to strike me down. Why shouldn't I just give Him my permission to do it?

After crying until I had no tears left, I shuffled home by moonlight.

As the months passed and the fights between Jimmy and me continued, I played out this scene again and again. The pattern was always the same: I accidentally tripped the trigger that sent Jimmy into a rage and he lashed out. I wept and I walked through the neighborhood believing that eventually he would come looking for me. When he didn't, I begged God to kill me.

Eventually when I'd had enough, my own anger kicked in and I ended the relationship. Then Jimmy came back.

Repeat cycle.

## From Sparks to a Bonfire

Absurd as it may sound, by our senior year we were discussing marriage. I don't think we ever considered the possibility that our unhealthy patterns of behavior would continue even after we said *I do*. If we thought about it at all, we simply assumed that somehow our love, with a little help from the marriage vows, would heal all wounds.

My parents, however, were not so naïve. When Jimmy and I graduated from high school and asked their permission to marry, they refused to give it. "No! Absolutely not! You cannot get married!" they fumed. "You're going to college!"

That didn't go well.

With our marriage plans on hold, we tried to figure out what to do next. While my parents intended to pay my college tuition and send me to a school they approved, Jimmy's parents couldn't afford to send him to college at all. "I'm going to have to get a job to pay my way to Texas Tech," he told me.

"If you're going to Tech, so am I."

When I informed my dad I wanted to attend Texas Tech, that conversation didn't go well either. He went off like a bottle rocket on the fourth of July. "You'll never go to the same college with Jimmy!" he said. "You'll never even be in the same town! I won't pay for it!"

The discussion deteriorated from there. We exchanged heated words and sparks flew, igniting a bonfire of emotion. When Dad slapped me across the side of the face, I packed my suitcase and left home for good.

I had no doubt that I could support myself. My parents had always required us to earn our own money and I'd been working at odd jobs for years. At seventeen, I'd started working part time at a bank and I still had that job. The bank hired me full time and I moved into a tiny duplex.

My parents eventually called a truce and I made peace with them, but I stayed in my duplex and continued to support myself. Jimmy moved to Lubbock and enrolled at Texas Tech. Heartsick over being apart, we spent most of our money talking long distance. By the time Jimmy finished his first year at Tech, we decided to get married. We were only 19 years old and my parents still weren't enthusiastic about the idea, but they realized they couldn't stop us so they agreed.

## *Would You Like to Wear Some Potatoes with That Meatloaf?*

Jimmy moved home from Texas Tech and started attending Amarillo College. Suddenly Jimmy wasn't the only one financially strapped. I felt the pinch too. So instead of spending money we didn't have going out on a date, I invited him to come to my house for dinner on Saturday evening. I spent the day cleaning until everything glistened; I went grocery shopping and made his favorite meal.

When he didn't show up on time I assumed he was just running a bit late. Expecting him to arrive any minute, I lit the candles and put the meatloaf, mashed potatoes, and green beans on the table. I paced for a while making sure everything was perfect. Then I made myself sit down and wait.

Half an hour later the food was cold.

I looked at the clock and realized Jimmy was 45 minutes late and hadn't bothered to call. My mind leapt like a gymnast from one possibility to another. What had happened? Had he forgotten? Had he been in a car wreck? Surely if he'd been in an accident his family would have let me know.

An hour after he'd said he would arrive for dinner, Jimmy sauntered in without an apology.

"Where have you been?" I asked.

He shrugged. "Playing golf."

"Why didn't you call me?"

"I don't have to call you!" he said, his eyes flashing. "And I don't like it when you nag me!"

Jimmy plopped down into a chair at the table waiting for me to serve him. I might have done it if I hadn't seen his expression. I'd never seen such a smug look on anyone's face. Not only was he unapologetic, he was actually pleased with himself for having put me in my place.

Looking at the ruined meal and Jimmy's surly demeanor, I felt a bewildering ferocity rise up in me. This was the man I'd given up a college education for? This was the guy that had cost me a relationship with my parents?

I didn't think; I reacted. I dumped the mashed potatoes over his head. *"Karen!"* he screamed. I followed it with the green beans and the meatloaf. *"Karen! What are you doing?"*

"I'm out of here!" I said as I grabbed my keys and ran outside.

His car had blocked the driveway so I drove through the backyard sideswiping the clothesline before making it to the alley and speeding away. I was furious. I'd rather live alone for the rest of my life than be with a man who'd treat me that way.

His attitude horrified me. He'd been thrilled to use that situation to show me who was boss. Alarm shot through my veins, giving me a wakeup call that tempted me to end the relationship for good.

But as usual, Jimmy came back apologetic. And as usual, I accepted his apology and took him back. And our plans to get married were still on.

## Bachelor Party Betrayal

A week before the wedding, Jimmy's friends held a bachelor party for him. I knew they'd get drunk but he promised me that no members of the opposite sex would be invited.

"I've already told them no girls," he said.

The night of his bachelor party I went out with friends. The next day Jimmy called and I asked how it went. "It was great," he said. He was quiet but I didn't think much about it.

"So, no girls?"

"No girls," he said. "We got drunk and played poker."

Later that day one of my friends called and she was steamed. "Do you know what they did last night?" she asked.

"No, what?"

"There were girls!"

"There were? Jimmy didn't tell me that."

I had one cardinal rule: don't lie to me. Jimmy knew my position on that. I'd told him time and again, "No matter what you do, always tell me the truth."

I pondered the situation and decided to give Jimmy the benefit of the doubt.

He called me the next night. "Hey, I need to tell you something."

"Okay."

"I wasn't being completely honest."

I was so happy that he was coming clean with me that my heart did a little dance. He admitted that there were girls at the party.

Then he added, "There were girls. And I had sex with one of them."

"Wait…what?"

"I had sex with her."

In an instant, every shred of love and trust between us splintered into a lightshow of pain. I felt shattered. Violated. Betrayed at the most primal level. Too shaken to speak, I struggled in silence to steady my voice.

"You know what?" I said. "I can't marry you. The wedding is off."

After three years of a toxic relationship, we never even made it to divorce court.

We'd crashed and burned before the wedding.

# CHAPTER THREE

*A Fractured Foundation*

# 03

## A Fractured Foundation

Late that night someone knocked on the door of my little duplex. I didn't need to look; I knew it was Jimmy. "I'm not going to open the door!" I called.

"Karen, *please!*"

Unmoved, I stood inside with my arms crossed. Then I heard something strange, like an animal strangling on a bone. Looking out the window, I saw Jimmy on his knees…sobbing. You'd have to know Jimmy to realize how the sight shocked me.

He never, ever cried. Not over physical pain and certainly not over emotional pain. Yet as I watched through the window he sobbed and sobbed. In the four years that we'd dated, I'd only seen him truly devastated once, when his grandfather died. I'd never seen anything like this.

I opened the door and let him come inside. Tears streamed down his face and his eyes were red and puffy. This wasn't the Jimmy I knew. "Karen," he said, "I don't deserve to be married to you; I know that. I don't blame you for not marrying me. But I want you to know I'm totally repentant. I'm not just sorry for what I did to you, I've repented to God and begged for His forgiveness. With or without you, I've turned my heart and my life over to God."

As many times as we'd broken up, Jimmy himself had never been broken. He'd been miserable, but not repentant. This time something different had happened—and I could tell the tears were the least of it. Jimmy had experienced a real encounter with God. He'd changed. It was all over him. I couldn't deny it.

Seeing that, it was easy for me to forgive him. "If God can forgive you, so can I."

Time proved me right about Jimmy; he was born again that day. I'd been born again in high school so we were both new creatures in Christ. Of course, this didn't mean we were automatically healed from our emotional wounds or delivered from our dysfunctional patterns of behavior. We weren't. But as we moved forward with our plans to marry, I found Jimmy to be softer and more tenderhearted.

My parents didn't have the money to throw us a big wedding. They'd been going through a financially rough time. The best they could do was have the ceremony at their house and ask the pastor of their church to officiate. One of their friends played the piano and others prepared the food. Because of my parent's financial situation and our desire to keep our wedding simple it was very small. The only people who attended were immediate family.

We spent the little bit of money we'd saved and the $100 my dad gave us to drive to Colorado Springs for our honeymoon. Afterwards we settled into a different duplex we'd rented together. It was a disgusting place that we hated from the start. Every time we turned on the lights at night cockroaches scattered in every direction.

Otherwise, however, those early days of marriage were like heaven on earth. We were still in the honeymoon phase and, having spent a year apart, we were thrilled to be together every day. Jimmy even decided his friends were a bad influence on him and made the tough decision to leave them behind, which I respected.

Two weeks after our wedding another amazing thing happened. Jimmy had a profound encounter with God. He spoke to Jimmy in a vision and told him, "You'll be speaking to multitudes some day." We hadn't yet found a church and emotionally we were still a mess, but both Jimmy and I were both so spiritually simple and childlike it didn't occur to us to question his experience.

Jimmy had a beautiful voice and was gifted in music. He played the guitar and wrote his own songs, which I never tired of hearing. We wouldn't have been surprised if God had called him into a music ministry. But we never imagined He would call him to preach.

From the beginning, however, we only wanted God's will. And whatever Jimmy was called to do, I wanted with all my heart to be a support and a help to him. So we just took God at His word and believed Him.

One thing that did start to bother us, though, was the ungodly environment Jimmy had to deal with at his job. He worked at a car wash surrounded by guys who cursed all day and partied hard at night. The atmosphere made Jimmy so miserable he finally quit and went to work selling appliances at his uncle's store.

## *Sex and Marriage*

The most surprising thing about marriage for me was Jimmy's seemingly insatiable appetite for sex. I liked sex but he was ready to go morning, noon and night, every single day. It boggled my mind. I never refused him but one day I did say, "Do you always have to…?"

I thought it was a legitimate question. He didn't. It hit his rejection button and resulted in a bad fight. Just like when we were dating, I fully accepted blame. "Okay! Okay! I'm sorry," I said. "It was totally my fault."

We'd been married seven months and had just moved again into a rented house. We were lying in bed one morning when I said, "You know it would be so fun to have kids!"

"Yeah!" Jimmy agreed. Until then, we'd been careful to use protection. The first time we had sex without it, I got pregnant.

With my parents living in Dallas and Jimmy's parents at work all the time, we had no support system. It was a hard pregnancy and I was only 19. Yet those challenges didn't scare me.

Although I was emotionally dependent, I was very independent in every other way. I'd never been the kind of woman who worried about having somebody to look after me. I knew I could earn a living, work full time, mow the lawn, clean the house, and take care of a baby—all by myself, if I had to. I didn't need other people to help me survive.

What I did need, however, was an emotional connection.

When Jimmy and I were dating, the thing I'd loved about our relationship had been our communication. He and I had talked about everything, which was very fulfilling to me. But a few months after we married, he just shut down.

I don't know why it is, but it seems that some men, once they say their vows, are done talking. Jimmy turned out to be one of those men. He was getting what he wanted from me—which was sex—anytime he wanted it. But what I wanted and needed from him, he'd stopped giving.

That drove the first wedge in our already wobbly foundation.

## Cracks in the Relationship

Jimmy's parents started their own appliance store and hired him to work for them. By the time our daughter Julie was born I was helping out too, a few hours a week. We had also moved again into a new apartment. Driven by their strong work ethic, Jimmy's parents took almost no time off and they expected the same from him. Sometimes it seemed as though they were going to work him to death, and that put even more stress on our relationship.

During this time we were able to purchase a home that was available through government subsidies. Even though it was very small and twenty miles away it fit our budget and was much better than the apartment we were living in. Soon after that I became pregnant with our son Brent. Before he was born we decided to sell our government-subsidized house and move closer to Jimmy's work. Fortunately, we made money on the house and it was a big blessing.

Unfortunately, I had Brent on the week our house sale closed and we had to move while I was in the hospital. Because the tight time frame of the sale of our house and the closing, we weren't able to find a new home before I went into labor. So while I was in the hospital having our son, Brent, Jimmy had to buy a new home without me seeing it and move us before I left the hospital. It was a lot of pressure to say the least.

After leaving the hospital and coming directly to our new home the stress began to intensify. I started to feel overwhelmed. I had with a new baby and was recovering from having a C-Section, a strong-willed three year-old, and a husband who'd shut down and wouldn't talk. If that weren't bad enough, my weight was out of control. I'd always struggled with it, but I'd gained seventy pounds during my second pregnancy.

    I was miserable.

I looked in the mirror one morning and didn't know the person staring back at me. "You can be miserable or you can change this," I said to myself.

Fed up with misery, I opted to change. I decided to stop comforting myself with food and using it to gain affirmation. When I'd lived with my parents, they'd praised me for my cooking and that had made me want to cook even more. Since cooking made me love to eat, it had always been a vicious cycle.

But no more. I was determined. Those days were over.

Trading my recipes for an exercise routine, I started jogging. It hammered my joints and made me feel as though my insides were falling out. I tried walking 45 minutes a day instead but that accomplished nothing. My weight remained the same.

I increased the time to an hour three days a week. Again, nothing changed. I finally realized I would have to walk an hour—every day.

Sugar was never my thing but I'd always loved potatoes. So I set strict limits. I told myself, "No Karen, you can't have potatoes every night for dinner." As I struggled to get and keep the pounds off, I discovered I couldn't do it by just exercising and giving up potatoes. In time, I had to say no to white flour as well.

One thing I appreciated about Jimmy is this: As I alternately failed and succeeded in my attempts to get in shape, he never criticized my body. He never griped about my weight. He didn't complain about my butt or my relatively flat chest. Regardless of my physical imperfections or the scars that marred me, Jimmy always thought I was beautiful. I was grateful for that.

But I longed for something more.

Since I could no longer turn to food, I wanted the comfort that came from the closeness Jimmy and I had once shared. But it wasn't there anymore. He worked almost nonstop, and when he did have time off he spent it golfing. He had nothing left for me and the kids. Yet when he walked in the door, he expected June Cleaver to be standing there waiting for him with a smile and an apron.

He expected the kids to be perfect and the house to be spotless. He was such a perfectionist that right after we married he actually taught me how he wanted me to clean the house. As far as he was concerned, his way was the *right* way.

Because I love to serve, I worked hard to keep the house like he wanted it. But he didn't respond the way I'd hoped. When he finally got home in the evenings, no matter what was going on, he collapsed in front of the TV, picked up the remote, and checked out.

One day after work, he came by the house to pick up his clubs on the way to the golf course and I dared to say something about it. "Jimmy, can't you just stay home with us and not golf today?" I asked.

He didn't even have to think about his answer. "Let me tell you something Karen," he said. "I resent coming home and having you put all your expectations on me! I'm working as hard and I can and I need some support from you!"

Brent was crying and dinner was cold because Jimmy had worked late and hadn't bothered to call. I looked around at all I had to deal with and said, "You know, I need some support from you too, Jimmy. I understand that you work hard. That was okay for a year or two, but when is it our turn? Brent needs you. Julie needs you. I need you. You've been gone for three years! When do we get you back?"

That started another battle. "I'm not at all interested in playing less golf!" Jimmy said as he walked out and slammed the door.

When he got home that night he slept on the sofa. As usual, I cried myself to sleep. The cold war dragged on for days until I finally gave up and apologized.

## *Life with an Alpha Male*

We attended a good church but nothing we heard from the pulpit made a difference in what was happening at home. Weeks turned into months and Jimmy's attitude remained the same: He didn't want to talk to me anymore, but he did want to come home from playing golf each day to a pristine house, a good meal, quiet children, passionate sex, and a compliant wife.

I thought maybe if we prayed together God would help us work out our relationship. "Jimmy, would you please pray with me?" I begged.

"No! How many times do I have to tell you, I'd rather pray alone?"

Then he went off on one of his tirades.

Jimmy had been an emotional brute before we married. Now he was a full-blown bully. A hard-core chauvinist, he believed it was a man's job to run things and a woman's job to obey him. He had no desire to communicate with me. He just wanted me to listen when he talked. The last thing he wanted was to hear my thoughts or opinions.

Given his family history, his perspective made sense. The Evans men had traditionally been proud, rugged men who overcame adversity by pulling themselves up by their own bootstraps. They didn't need help from anybody. What they needed was for everyone to get out of their way so that they could do what had to be done. When trouble arose they gritted their teeth and plowed through it—alone.

Jimmy, following in their footsteps, was the ultimate lone wolf alpha male. And that kind of man doesn't cater to women. He certainly didn't help out at home and never changed a diaper.

I'd married him believing that the love we felt for each other would solve all our problems and that, in spite of his inner struggles, Jimmy would try to meet my needs just as I tried to meet his. But nothing could have been farther from the truth. From the very earliest years of our marriage, he simply ruled the roost, telling me what to do, bullying me with his words, and leaving me emotionally bankrupt.

When I hit my limit I did what I'd always done—I got mad. I slammed cupboards, jumped in the car and squealed tires as I fled from our house. I sobbed and cried, as if trying to wash away the pain of his razor sharp words that sliced through my soul.

The old breakup game wasn't an option for me anymore; I was a married woman with two children. All I could do was withdraw emotionally, so I did…and he did too. We spent days at a time not speaking and not sleeping in the same room.

Not once did he ever apologize. The standoff always continued until I said *I'm sorry* and took responsibility for our problems. That was our new cycle. He battered me emotionally until I ran sobbing from the house. Then I suffered his cold silence until I relented and apologized.

Repeat cycle.

## *No Leaning Allowed*

I stood in the kitchen one morning feeling as if I'd just run a marathon. Julie stared at me like a mini version of Jimmy and said, "Don't tell me what to do!" Brent, showing all the symptoms of having strep throat again, couldn't stop crying.

I'd been awake for so long that my eyes felt like sandpaper. I was past exhausted trying to make breakfast. The laundry had piled up and Jimmy snapped at me about it before storming off to work. The kitchen was a mess and, unable to quiet my fussy kids, I just wanted to fall on the floor and wail with them. Instead, I started a load of laundry and went to work on the house.

The day passed in a blur of exhaustion as Brent's symptoms worsened. That afternoon when I was thawing something for dinner, one of my friends called and hurt my feelings. My mother phoned and we had a fight. I put dinner on the table where it grew cold. As usual, Jimmy didn't bother letting me know he was working late.

Somehow I got through the evening and managed to get both kids to bed. I'd just started cleaning up the kitchen when Jimmy strolled in. He wanted sex.

## *One More Round*

He either didn't see my exhaustion or didn't care. Who knows? Maybe the lecture he'd given me that morning was supposed to be foreplay. Of course, I would never deny him. So, drawing on my last trace of energy, I switched off the light and headed for the bedroom. Afterwards he turned over and went to sleep. Tears streaming down my face, I got up and finished washing the dinner dishes and let my thoughts torment me again about how horrible I was.

Jimmy wasn't clueless about what was happening. He knew, just as I did, that we had marital problems but he didn't know what to do about them. He truly believed I was completely to blame for them all.

I coped by trying to handle everything on my own. When I did approach Jimmy with any kind of need, he stonewalled me. He shut down and shut me out even more than usual. If I pushed, the verbal abuse started and continued until I was reeling with rage and rejection.

One reason I tended to let his behavior go until I couldn't take it anymore was because I understood that he was under a lot of pressure. He was trying to provide for the family and keep his parents happy at work at the same time.

Being in control of things was what made Jimmy feel at peace. So when I pushed him he reacted by fighting to get me back under his control. Although we never argued around the children, I knew they picked up on the tension between us. I felt so guilty and condemned about it that after our fights I turned inward and sank even deeper into depression.

Each time it happened, I felt like I was drifting farther away from the relationship with God I so desperately wanted and needed. Drowning in self-hatred, I became ever more convinced that the way my husband treated me reflected the way God felt about me too.

The kids were in bed one evening while Jimmy and I sat at the kitchen table discussing our finances. We were at a stalemate, with conflicting opinions about how we should handle our money. He wanted to spend it while I wanted to save it.

If I'd kept my thoughts to myself, things wouldn't have escalated. But I had the audacity to open my mouth. When I began to explain my perspective, Jimmy's anger roared to life and he slapped me down

with a single sentence. "Either you change…or else!" he threatened.
</p>
End of discussion.

I felt like a featherweight boxer who'd been knocked out by Mohammad Ali in the first round. I stumbled to the bed and stared, sleepless, at the ceiling. Not only was I not an equal partner in this marriage, I wasn't even allowed to have an opinion different than his.

I felt as though all the life was being sucked out of me.

# CHAPTER FOUR

*Spontaneous Combustion*

# 04

*Spontaneous Combustion*

When the tears finally came it seemed as though I was going to drown in them. I pulled myself out of bed and stumbled to the closet. Slipping inside, I shut the door and sobbed until there was nothing left. Some people, I realized, drank when they were upset. Some people took drugs. Some people comforted themselves with food. I couldn't even let myself do that anymore. My only relief was to cry until I was spent.

I crawled back into our empty bed feeling wrung out. Even an ocean of tears couldn't cleanse me from the guilty sense that Jimmy was right and everything really was my fault. I had ruined our marriage. For every fight, every tear, and every hurt—I alone was to blame.

More than anything I wanted to kill myself. I needed relief from the pain and Jimmy needed to be free of me. But down the hall two children slept in the assurance that when they woke up, I would be there for them.

I couldn't kill myself.

But I couldn't end my marriage either. I knew God hated divorce and that left me in a state of utter and complete hopelessness. With no way to stop the pain, life stretched before me like a boundless desert of despair. I saw no end to it.

I stiffened and turned away when Jimmy came to bed. We lay there back to back as anger shimmered between us like heat off a sidewalk on a sizzling summer day. I hoped against hope that he would say something. Apologize. Tell me everything would be all right. Just pull me close and hold me.

Within minutes he was snoring.

Seriously? I thought. You can go to bed and sleep?

I decided not to give him the satisfaction of finding me there at his side when he woke up. I inched out from under the covers in such tiny increments that the mattress didn't move. Slipping out of bed, I tiptoed into the living room where I huddled in the darkness and begged God to change me.

The next morning, Jimmy's jaw was clenched and his eyes were cold. He didn't speak and I knew he wouldn't until I took responsibility for what I'd done. But I dug in my heels. For days neither of us said a word to the other. Stubborn and silent, I went about my life, taking care of the kids, cooking and cleaning and doing everything as if he wasn't there.

Even though we weren't talking about it, the argument we'd had went around and around my mind like a broken record. Jimmy said this and I said that. The disparity in the way we viewed the same event left me feeling crazy. Was I nuts?

Finally, Jimmy came home one evening and said, "We need to talk about this."

Dread dropped like a rock into my stomach. I hated those words. I hated the pretense that we were going to talk. There would be no talking; just Jimmy scolding and me listening. This was going to be another long session of him picking me apart and arguing that every problem in our marriage was my fault.

I'd realized over the years that his tone of voice hurt even more than his words. He often yelled, as if getting louder would give him more control over me; and his tone was angry, judgmental, and mean.

Ignoring the ache in my gut, I tried to believe this time would be different. Maybe, for once, we'd both take responsibility for the problem.

Of course that's not what happened.

"You can't talk to me that way," He shouted. "It's not right and you have no idea how it makes me feel. You're a rebellious, disobedient wife!"

"Jimmy, you need to listen to what you say to me! If only we had a recorder and you could play back our conversations!"

"You're not taking responsibility for your behavior," he insisted.

Refuting my arguments, he pounded home his points like a prosecutor proving his case. He droned on and on until I grew weary of hearing it. Just admit you're wrong, I told myself.

"I'm sorry," I said. "I know I was wrong."

## The Shame of Behaving Badly

As soon as I repented he forgave me and it was over. For all of our problems, there were a few things that Jimmy and I got right and one of those was forgiving. Some people spend a lifetime never understanding the power of forgiveness, but Jimmy and I got that lesson down.

We wouldn't allow each other to wallow in unforgiveness, resentment, or offence, regarding any situation. If someone hurt my feelings, I could talk about it with Jimmy and vent my emotions, giving all the reasons why I felt hurt. But then I had to forgive. We taught our kids to do the same thing; we never allowed them to stay mad.

I believe God honored that in our relationship because it kept the seeds of bitterness from taking root. It stopped us from completely ruining our lives. In spite of the fact that we had plenty of reasons to justify our anger and offenses, we knew that left unchecked they would destroy us.

Of course, when it came to our marriage, Jimmy didn't think he needed any forgiveness. From his perspective, he'd never done anything wrong; he'd never messed up and all of our fights were my fault. So I did all the repenting and he did all the forgiving.
He was big that way.
    Just saying.

When it came to my temper tantrums he truly did have a lot to forgive. When I got fed up with feeling like the fall guy for all of our problems, I slammed doors. I screamed. I ran to the car and screeched down the street at a hundred miles an hour. I was gone for hours at a time. Sometimes I left in the middle of a fight. Other times I stormed out of the house in the middle of the night.

I behaved so horrifically that when I cooled off, shame engulfed me. Drowning in condemnation over the disgraceful way I'd acted, I had to face once again what I believed but hated to admit: There was something so wrong with me that I was the root of all the evil in our lives. I was unlovable. My parents hadn't known what to do with me. My husband didn't know what to do with me. God couldn't even stand me.

Don't get me wrong; I loved God. But I knew better than to think that He loved me. At best He tolerated me and I wondered how long that would last.

## *Out of Control*

Things settled down for a while and then the cycle would repeat. Each time it did, I always ended up running to the car and driving away. For years I didn't know what it was about our fights that made me want to get my hands on the wheel of a car, but I suspect it was because I needed to feel in control of something.

At home, I didn't even have control over how I cleaned the house. Everything had to be done Jimmy's way. But alone in the car no one could tell me what to do. I could go anywhere I wanted. I could drive as fast as I wanted. I could be gone for as long as I wanted. When I climbed into the car and drove, I felt like I was in charge.

It was the one time I got to have my way.

What a blessed relief.

It was odd, really, that driving became my solace because the greatest fear in my life was that I would die in a car wreck. I never suffered from a fear of heights. I wasn't afraid of flying. I wasn't afraid of animals. I'd had dreams of horrible tornadoes, but I didn't die in them. I was only afraid of dying in a car wreck.

Which, I may as well admit, was why I hated the way Jimmy drove.

My mother was a very aggressive driver and she taught me to drive like she did. She trained me to stay focused and alert, to drive as fast as the speed limit allowed, and to know all the shortcuts. Jimmy didn't drive that way. He often got distracted and didn't pay attention, and he often chose meandering, inefficient routes.

As soon as he got behind the wheel, my anxiety levels soared. I braced myself while he drove. When he got distracted, my fear intensified. If I made a comment about his speed or suggested a possible shortcut, it infuriated him.

It's no wonder some of our worst fights were in the car. Jimmy's anger at a woman telling him what to do collided with my terror of car accidents and we spontaneously combusted. We'd done it ever since that first drive to Colorado Springs on our honeymoon. Even if we were just driving across town, by the time we reached our destination we were often so emotionally wrecked we weren't speaking.

## A Stoney Face and a Hard Heart

As time passed, I allowed my heart to harden against Jimmy and it showed in my expression. When he walked in the house, the first thing he saw was the misery on my face, etched there as if in stone, like the Presidents on Mount Rushmore. Hard and cold and brittle, I looked as though my face would crack if I tried to smile. Sometimes just seeing me was enough to make Jimmy want to fight.

I could see what was happening: the way his shoulders slumped when he saw me, the flash of pain in his eyes. I knew my very countenance was pushing him farther away from me and making everything worse. But I didn't know what to do about it.

"God," I begged, "help me change my face!"

I tried hard to smile when Jimmy came home, and when I managed it, I considered that a huge victory. I also watched how other couples we knew interacted. I noticed the wives greeted their husbands with kindness. "I'm so happy to see you!" they'd say—and they actually meant it. I saw them call each other and their children Sweetie, Babe or Honey.

Neither Jimmy nor I had grown up in families that used endearments and we thought they were ridiculous. We always laughed about it in private saying, "Eww! That's so gross!" When I called the kids to dinner I said, "Hurry up!" I never called them sweet names.

As I studied the examples set by my friends, however, this started bothering me, so I started using endearments with our children. I also made some changes in how I spoke to Jimmy. In spite of everything, I loved him and wanted us to at least find peace, if not happiness. So I practiced saying nice things to him like, "You look tired. I can't imagine what kind of day you must've had."

Men aren't as high maintenance as we women are and those little things helped defuse many an argument. It made such a difference that I started doing other little things I thought he might appreciate. Like getting his socks folded first when I did the laundry so they'd always be ready for him to wear.

"I've got someone to watch the kids," I said one day. "I thought I'd just ride in the golf cart while you play." In an instant his face went from flint to tender. He loved having me ride around in the cart. While none of those things changed our underlying issues, they made our life less stressful.

Still, it seemed inevitable that something would set us off. So before long that's what happened.

I'd had one of those harried days every mother experiences. The kids had been unmanageable and my patience had worn thin. When Jimmy walked in the door after work I was trying to clean the kitchen and get dinner on the table. He looked around, took in the whole scene, and then dropped onto the sofa and vegged out in front of the television.

Rather than communicating to him what I needed and asking him to help with the kids, I seethed. As far as I was concerned, I shouldn't have to ask. He could see what was happening. He should have figured out by himself that I needed a hand. While he watched TV, I worked in the kitchen like a bull in the ring with a matador, steam coming out of my ears and practically pawing the floor in anger.

Jimmy ignored me so I stopped what I was doing to deal with the kids myself.

"Would you mind taking the trash out?" I asked.

"Yeah, I'll get to it," he said but he didn't.

For a few minutes I slammed cupboards and whacked pans against the stove. Then I erupted, "Fine! I'll take care of everything myself!"

"What's wrong with you!" he screamed. "I know when the trash needs to be taken out!"

Repeat cycle.

## Lessons from the Fiery Furnace

Although the messages we were hearing at church didn't directly impact our marriage, they did help me personally. I still remember one sermon in particular the pastor preached from the book of Daniel. He told the story about the three young Hebrew boys that were ordered by the king to bow down to a huge golden statue.

If they didn't do it, the pastor explained, they'd be sentenced to death. The king would have them thrown into a fiery furnace. But they refused to bow. Instead they said to the king, "Look, we believe that our God will deliver us out of your fire. But know this: Even if He doesn't, we'd rather die than be disloyal to Him."

I was such a wimp it was incredible to me that those three teenagers were that zealous for the Lord. They'd never seen Him. They didn't have a personal relationship with Him. But they made a decision to serve Him regardless. They said that even if God didn't rescue them they'd still be faithful to Him.

I loved that!

It reminded me of how I felt toward God: I didn't really know Him, either. Yet I felt such a zeal for Him that I wouldn't deny Him. Even as a child I had determined to be faithful to Him regardless of my circumstances.

Sitting in that service, I realized that God had to be my first priority. If He never saved my marriage, I would serve Him. If I was unhappy until the day I died, I couldn't walk away from Him. He was in me. From that day my hunger and thirst for God increased and I set my heart on doing whatever the Bible said for me to do, without questioning it.

At home, while cleaning and cooking, I developed the habit of watching Christian television. On one broadcast I learned that in the book of Malachi God said we should tithe and give. A few weeks later

Jimmy and I attended a church where the pastor preached on the same thing. When we arrived home I told Jimmy I liked the pastors message and wanted to give some money to the church.

"We can't give money," Jimmy explained. "We're poor."

"But look here in Malachi. God said if we give ten percent, everything will be okay. We just need to trust God." Even though Jimmy disagreed he allowed me to give to the church. Before long, we noticed our appliances stopped breaking. Our cars didn't break down and we were more financially blessed.

Our marriage, however, was another matter. Although neither of us said the words out loud, we both wondered if we would end up in divorce court. I'd read in Malachi 2:16 that God says, "The man who hates and divorces his wife does violence to the one he should protect." I meditated on that and realized that God was saying that divorce not only brings violence into the home, but it also brings violence to our society. Convicted, I wondered if there was a way we could save our marriage without sacrificing our sanity.

## *Seeking the Lord*

During this time we met some new friends in church who would become very important to us. It was a couple who were our age and had children the same ages as ours. The husband was a golfer like Jimmy and they hit it off instantly. He became the first Christian man Jimmy ever got close to as a friend. She became one of my dearest friends who taught me a lot about the Lord.

As we got closer to them they began taking us to some special worship services at a camp outside of town. We had never experienced anything like it. It was wonderful and the music was unlike anything we had ever heard. Both Jimmy and I were deeply touched by it and it began a season in our lives of seeking the Lord as never before.

One night after returning from one of those services I went to bed but Jimmy stayed up and prayed for several hours. The Lord was doing a deep work in his heart and I was overjoyed. But at the same time I wondered how the Lord could do something like that for Jimmy when he could be so hurtful to me with his mouth and treat me with such disrespect.

And then I began wondering if maybe I was the problem and God was somehow punishing me. This was just another part of the cycle that kept repeating. No matter if things were good or bad I interpreted everything through the lens of self-hate.

# CHAPTER FIVE

*The Search for Answers*

# 05

## *The Search for Answers*

I curled into a fetal position on the sofa and sobbed for what seemed like hours. Jimmy had called home and lacerated me—again—with his words. Each time he did it I felt like less of a person. If I didn't escape I was afraid there would soon be nothing left of me.

*I can't do this anymore,* I thought.

I pulled myself off the couch and started packing for the kids and me. I didn't know what I was going to do or where I would live; I just knew I couldn't live this way any longer. Going home was out of the question. When I married, my mother let me know that regardless of the problems I encountered in my relationship with Jimmy, I could never go home again.

I thought of calling our Sunday School teachers, Kerm and Lou Ethel, a couple we looked up to. We'd gotten to know them and they might be willing to help. I dialed their phone number while continuing to pack.

"Lou Ethel," I said when she answered, "I'm leaving Jimmy. Do you have any idea where the kids and I could go?"

"Don't do anything!" she said. "I'll come right over."

"There's no need for you to do that," I replied. "I've made up my mind. I'm not doing this anymore."

A few minutes later, Jimmy called. "I'm leaving," I told him. "I've already packed my suitcases."

Furious, he came home. He started arguing with me and trying to talk me out of leaving. It was then that I told him I had called Lou Ethel and told her everything. He was horrified that I'd called and aired our dirty laundry in front of her.

Shortly after that we received a call from Lou Ethel asking us to go out to eat dinner with her and Kerm. Even though Jimmy was very uncomfortable we went.

We met them at the restaurant and made small talk for a few awkward minutes. Then Kerm started talking. "Jimmy," Kerm said, "I used to be just like you. Lou Ethel and I have been through things like this, too."

*What?*

Jimmy and I stared at him in shock. He might as well have said they'd roller skated to the moon. It was impossible. Kerm adored Lou Ethel and they had the kind of marriage we envied. They could never have been anything like us.

We sat, stunned, as Kerm talked about how stubborn, prideful, and dominating he'd once been. He even called his behavior sin. Both he and Lou Ethel talked with openness and honesty about all the problems they'd had in their marriage and how they'd solved them.

Listening to their story, we found what we'd lost—hope.

I agreed to stay and try to work things out.

## *A Divine Appointment*

I stood behind the counter, helping out at Jimmy's parents' appliance store, when a man walked in carrying a broken television. Jimmy was with another customer so I waited on him. As we visited, he mentioned he was the pastor of Trinity Fellowship.

"We've heard so much about Trinity!" I said. "We've even talked about visiting there."

"Why don't you come this Wednesday night?"

We did and eventually joined the church.

The pastor and his wife were wonderful and the people there were nice but there was one problem. When I was around them my excruciating shyness ratcheted up about a thousand notches. In part, this was due to being in a new situation, but that wasn't all of it. We'd heard great things about the way the Lord was moving in the church. But even though that was good in my mind it meant I didn't measure up spiritually to their level. What would they think of someone like me?

This issue was so troubling to me that eventually I made an appointment with the pastor and told him what was going on. He was very kind and said some things that helped me. At the end of our time, I knelt in his office as he laid his hands on me and prayed. It was a very comforting experience.

But still, nothing changed in our marriage.

The fights raged on. The tears continued to flow. I slammed cabinet doors and sped away in the car.

I didn't know what to do. My marriage was miserable but I didn't feel right about getting a divorce. It appeared that God wasn't going to kill me and take me out of the situation any time soon and I'd reached a point of desperation. I couldn't live with all my fears and anxieties. At times I felt almost paralyzed by them. I knew my insecurities were robbing me, not only of friends but of living my life to the fullest.

I'd gotten tired of going to women's conferences and feeling insecure because I didn't know what they were talking about. They acted like they knew God. I loved the Lord, but I didn't know Him. I felt as though I was living a lie. I went to church and acted spiritual but I had no personal knowledge of Jesus.

Okay…the truth was actually worse than that: I didn't even like the Jesus I read about in the Gospels.

Everyone talked about Him being sweet and kind, but that's not what I saw when I read about Him. I saw a Jesus who was always mad, especially at the Pharisees. When dealing with them He looked to me to be aloof, sad, and disappointed. He even said mean things to them.

I shuddered at verses like, *"Woe to you, scribes and Pharisees, hypocrites! For you are like whitewashed tombs which on the outside appear beautiful, but inside they are full of dead men's bones and all uncleanness."*

I felt certain that's what Jesus would say to me.

I didn't identify with the little children in the Gospels who sat in Jesus' lap and received His blessing. I didn't see myself as one of the disciples He chose to be His friends. I identified with the lepers. Sometimes I felt as though I was so bad that I needed to stay away from other people.

Other times, I saw myself as the Syrophoenician woman who asked God to heal her child. Jesus told her that granting her request would be like throwing the children's bread to the dogs. She replied, "Yes, Lord, but even the dogs under the table feed on the children's crumbs." That described how I felt: like a dog groveling around under Jesus' table, hoping to eat the crumbs.

Still, I didn't know where to find help except in the Bible, so I committed myself to read it and search for answers. Although I'd always read the Bible in bits and pieces, I told God, "Now I'm going to read the whole thing from beginning to end. I'm going to read it all the time and I'm not going to stop."

I had no idea at the time that decision was the hinge upon which every problem in my life would turn.

In the beginning, I approached the Bible with all my defenses on high alert. One reason I'd never read it all the way through was because some of it seemed so unbelievable to me. For instance, one scripture said that we were fearfully and wonderfully made. I knew better. Some people might have been made that way, but not me. I was a mess.

In the past when I'd bumped up against such seeming contradictions, I might have just shut the Bible and gotten busy doing something else. This time I wouldn't let myself do that. I was determined not only to keep reading—but to believe what I read.

What I didn't realize at the time, of course, was that like most people I'd always viewed the Bible through the lens of my own experience and feelings. For example, I had no real concept of grace, so I felt condemned when I read Galatians. Missing the whole point of the book, I thought, *Oh my, I've broken God's law and somebody has bewitched me! I've got to keep repenting of all my sins. I've got to figure out how to act the right way. Maybe if I pray enough, and read the Bible enough, and act good enough, then I'll experience His love.*

What's more, as a young Christian I'd always found the Bible confusing. I'd start reading in Genesis and get stuck in the first few pages. I couldn't even grasp the verses about us being created in God's image.

If I was confused in the very first book of the Bible, what hope was there for me?

Very little, it seemed.

But regardless, I kept my commitment to read the whole Bible all the way through. Instead of giving up, I persevered even through my confusion. And that changed my life.

## *A Different View of Suffering*

Before long I fell in love with the Old Testament. I especially liked the Psalms because I identified with David. He suffered a lot of hardships and he actually cried about them. Just like me, the man wept in despair! Psalms 51 became my prayer.

*Clean my heart Lord and make me new.*

It startled me to realize that a man like David would suffer the way he did. I'd always assumed I suffered pain because there was something wrong with me. Reading through the Psalms and delving into classic books by men like Andrew Murray, George McDonald and St. Francis of Assisi, I got a different perspective. As I saw how those incredible men suffered and yet still pursued God, I felt inspired to do the same. "Okay," I said, "I'm going to be like them. I'm going to find God no matter how much I hurt."

That sounded good in theory but when Jimmy would come home and verbally slice me into ribbons I'd cry in agony. I couldn't see how I could go on living, much less seek God. Then I'd remember what those great men had pointed out.

Jesus wept.

He suffered not only the worst physical pain imaginable, but rejection and persecution from those He loved. Through their writings I saw His pain. Through their teachings I learned the truth of Hebrews 4:14-15:

> *Therefore, since we have a great high priest who has passed through the heavens, Jesus the Son of God, let us hold fast our confession. For we do not have a high priest who cannot sympathize with our weaknesses, but One who has been tempted in all things as we are, yet without sin. Therefore let us draw near with confidence to the throne of grace, so that we may receive mercy and find grace to help in time of need.*

The idea that Jesus cared—that He sympathized—soothed my heart like a balm. I read the verses over and over, soaking in the comfort they offered. But every time I looked at verse 15 it was as though it had been written in tongues. Seriously? We were to go before God's throne with confidence that He would help?

Of all the things I lacked, confidence had to be at the top of the list.

I loved God but I had no confidence in His love for me.

According to the Bible, the fear of the Lord is the beginning of wisdom, so I should have been one of the wisest people on earth. That's how afraid I was of God. I'd been serious when I'd prayed He would send someone to kill me. I truly thought He'd do it. That's how I thought He felt about me.

But as I read through the Old Testament, I realized that there are two very different ways to fear the Lord. The Bible teaches us to fear Him in a positive sense, by deeply honoring, respecting, and loving Him. It teaches us to respond to His love for us by desiring more than anything to please Him.

The kind of fear I had for God was negative. I thought He was always mad at me. I believed in His sovereignty, His omnipotence, and His majesty, which is good, but in my world, if God showed up I'd better be on my face, otherwise He would be likely to crush me.

## *Paradigm Shift*

I curled up in my favorite chair as the morning sun peeked over the horizon and opened my Bible to the well-worn pages of Isaiah. Reading through the Old Testament in the early morning hours I'd discovered I liked that Book. Even though Isaiah's words pierced me, his heart seemed so kind.

I turned to Isaiah 30 and verse 15 seemed to jump off the page at me:

> *In quietness and confidence is your strength; but you'll have none of this.*

There was that word confidence again. Confidence, I realized, was lacking in my temperament. All my life I'd viewed myself through the eyes of other people, believing every negative word spoken against me: I was not smart. I was ugly. I was fat. I was pitifully shy. I was not wanted. I had no recognizable gifts.

From those beliefs, I'd created my own identity. I'd not only become self-conscious, I'd learned to despise myself. The only thing I felt confident about was what a horrible person I was.

> *"And therefore will the LORD wait," said Isaiah, "that he may be gracious unto you, and therefore will he be exalted, that he may have mercy upon you: for the Lord is a God of judgment: blessed are all they that wait for him"* (v. 18).

What a thought! God's desire was to be gracious and merciful to me. He wanted to bless me.

Some Christians may think of Isaiah as simply a fiery Old Testament prophet, but it was through his writings that I discovered how gracious and loving God was. In Isaiah I saw how much God loved a sinful, rebellious nation and how far God was willing to go in order to forgive and heal them. I saw Him search for someone who would help them. I read about Isaiah saying, "God, here I am! Use me!" and I so identified with him that I cried, "Me too, Lord! Use me!"

Isaiah revealed a God who didn't ask anything hard of those who'd sinned against Him. All He asked was that they return to Him—and rest in Him. Talk about an unfamiliar concept. I'd certainly never a pictured God who wanted us to come to Him and rest!

Reading Isaiah, I had a paradigm shift. For the first time I saw who God really is. And since Jesus is the manifestation of the Father, I got a revelation of Him as well. I saw that Jesus loved everybody—even those stubborn, rebellious Pharisees!—so much that He came to earth to pay for their sins; and that He, too, wanted people to come to Him and rest. Gradually, I realized I had misunderstood Jesus in the Gospels, and the New Testament started coming alive.

## *The Game Changer*

Before I got to the New Testament, however, I saw the Good News in the Old Testament. So, strange as it may sound, for me, reading the Old Testament all the way through was the game changer.

I learned about God's character there by reading about people like Abraham and Sarah. I identified with them, not because of their strong faith, but because they messed up a lot before they got it right. Sarah didn't trust that God could do what He said He would do, so she helped Him out by telling Abraham to sleep with her servant girl. That produced a baby all right, but Ishmael wasn't a part of God's plan.

In another instance, Abraham, the father of our faith, got scared that he would be killed because of Sarah's beauty. So he made her say that she was his sister! He let a wicked king take her away in order to save his own hide. Personally, I would have had a lot to say about that! Yet, Sarah called him Lord and did what he said.

Abraham and Sarah didn't do right all the time. They made really big mistakes. But they just kept on plodding along and doing their best to please God. As a result they are included in the Hebrews chapter twelve hall of faith. Abraham and Sarah persevered, and instead of rejecting them for their mistakes, God honored their faith.

The more I read the Bible, the more I fell in love with all the people I found in it. None of them, except Jesus, was perfect. They were all flawed. But as I watched God work with them, I saw that He wasn't looking to strike anyone down. He was always gracious and kind, patient and long suffering.

Over time, I went from being confused by the Bible to being intrigued, not just by what I found in it but by who I found there. People like Isaiah, David, Job, Joshua, Rahab, and Ruth fascinated and inspired me. As I read about them, they ceased to be flat, one dimensional characters. They became living, breathing people just like me, and I felt as though I knew them.

In every book of the Bible I saw some facet of God's personality revealed...and little by little, I felt myself relax. I realized He wasn't out to get me. He wasn't going to discard me as worthless because of my imperfections. He's a Redeemer!

I'd known women who read romance novels and fell just a little bit in love with the hero of the story.

Not me.

But as I slipped out of bed each morning, I hurried to my favorite chair as though headed for a tryst with a lover. The God I was discovering during my devotional times surpassed anything I'd ever imagined. I finally understood how it was that some people actually seemed to know Him. For those willing to persevere, God had revealed Himself on the pages of the Bible.

In those quiet morning hours as I met Him there, His perfect love began removing the fear and changing my heart. I would sit and just enjoy His amazing Presence.

# CHAPTER SIX

*The Power of Prayer*

## 06

*The Power of Prayer*

I felt like an impostor sitting in Bible study surrounded by women who all seemed to have it together. In comparison, my life was a mess. Even though I was discovering God on the pages of the Bible and seeing His nature in a new light, from a practical perspective I seemed to be making very little progress.

Each time I got my spiritual feet under me and gained some stability, Jimmy would go off on me and I'd lose ground, tumbling back into guilt and self-hatred. His tirades really messed with me. Although I truly loved the Lord and trusted Him more each day, I kept wondering, *Why would He let my husband speak to me that way unless He was just as upset with me?*

Instead of running to my closet to weep, I drove around begging for forgiveness. "Lord, I'm so sorry," I repeated over and over like a mantra. "I'm stubborn and stupid and disobedient. Oh Lord, *forgive* me."

At Bible study one day I stopped to talk to an older woman who recommended a book on how wives should pray for their husbands. I must have looked like a light bulb flashed on above my head. *I can pray! I can pray!* I thought as I left the meeting that day.

I bought the book and devoured it, praying the way it suggested. I also took to heart the counsel it offered about honoring your husband and treating him with love and respect even when he doesn't deserve it. That sounded so radical I figured it must be God. Certainly no woman would come up with such an idea on her own—especially if she had a jerk for a husband. *It's got to work!* I thought.

Although I was excited about implementing the plan, I soon discovered it was tougher than I'd expected. My old patterns of behavior were hard to overcome. When Jimmy yelled at me, the last thing I wanted to do was treat him with love and respect. I wanted to slam doors and run away…and sometimes I did. But each time I repented and tried again.

Over time I found it easier to stay with the program because of the way Jimmy reacted to it. He couldn't help but notice the stark contrast between my gentleness and the harsh way he treated me, and I enjoyed seeing the expression on his face when I reacted to his tirades with kindness. He looked like I'd just heaped hot coals on his head.

My enjoyment waned, however, when those hot coals failed to change his behavior.

Frustrated, I reasoned that if *he* wasn't changing I must be the problem. There must be something really bad-wrong with me. I would read Psalm 51 and camp there crying, "Oh God, create a clean heart in me! Make me a new person!" I didn't realize it at the time, but that prayer opened the door for God to go to work on my wrong thinking, anger, and abnormal insecurities. So as I prayed and continued to meditate on the Bible, little by little, an amazing thing happened.

I began to shift my eyes away from myself and onto God. I gave my attention to His Word, instead of focusing constantly on what was wrong with Jimmy and me.

Up to that point, I'd let our problems overshadow the power of God in my life. I'd allowed them to so obscure my vision that I couldn't see there were answers in the Bible. But as I spent more time reading God's Word, my perspective shifted and His power and promises started overshadowing my problems.

I stopped trying to talk to Jimmy about our situation (I'd finally learned we'd just end up in a fight) and talked to God instead, spending hours upon hours in prayer. I came out of those prayer times with newfound inner strength that helped me ignore Jimmy's dismissive attitude and smart remarks—at least, for one more day—and be more patient when he was vegging out in front of the TV refusing to engage with me and the kids.

In spite of the changes in my behavior, though, he basically stayed the same. He still railed at me and shut me out, and our marriage remained a train wreck. Having done everything I knew to do, I tried to decide if I should quit or keep going.

It would have been so easy to give up.

But as I stood at that dangerous crossroads and considered going back to my old ways, the Lord prompted me to consider my motives. Had I changed how I treated my husband just so he would give me what I wanted? Or had I done it because God required it of me? If it was the first, I had every right to quit; if the second, quitting wasn't an option.

In retrospect, I can see that God was drawing me to a deeper place with Him. He didn't want this to be just about my marriage. He wanted it to be about Him and me. He was after my heart.

## *The Lion at the Door*

"I'm not going to Life Group!" Jimmy shouted after a horrible fight.

"Well, I am," I replied. Not only did I need to be around other Christians, I needed to get out of that toxic environment. Jimmy stayed home sulking while I went to our group meeting.

"Where's Jimmy?" everyone asked.

"He's home…" I caught myself before saying that he was at home sucking his thumb and feeling sorry for himself.

"Karen," the Life Group leader said, "I was praying for you and Jimmy recently and I saw a huge lion at your house. It didn't attack you but it roared and roared at you from every doorway in your home. I feel like Satan is in your home trying to divide you and Jimmy and you've got to take control."

"Really?"

While I'd worked hard to change the way I responded to Jimmy's verbal abuse, I wasn't about to cover for him. According to the Bible, it's the truth that sets us free. I'd seen women try to hide verbal abuse, physical abuse, sexual abuse and other kinds of sin in their marriage, and it never did anyone any good. It actually made things worse.

I definitely couldn't afford for things to get worse, so I poured out the whole story. "Yes, we have been fighting a lot," I said.

The group leader responded with compassion and promised to pray for us.

"Good, we need prayer—a lot of it."

When I got home Jimmy asked, "What happened in Life Group?"

He was mortified when I told him.

"You what? You told them we'd been fighting? You need to keep our business private!"

"Jimmy, I don't care what you think. I'll tell anybody and everybody who'll listen. Besides, the group leader said Satan is in our home roaring and we've got to take control of the situation." Then I described the vision she'd seen.

Jimmy's eyes looked like saucers. "Oh my gosh!" he said. "That makes so much sense!"

We knew nothing about spiritual warfare back then, and it freaked us out a little to think a demon spirit was actually hanging around our home causing us to fight. But it also helped us in a powerful way. For the first time in our marriage Jimmy and I understood that we weren't just fighting with one another. We were under enemy assault — and the devil was doing everything in his power to destroy us.

I looked in Jimmy's eyes and saw a revelation dawning: He did have an enemy, but it wasn't me.

## *A Lonely Prophet and a Spiritual Chiropractor*

It helped that we were getting some revelation about what was going on. But even so, loneliness still ate at me day and night as Jimmy continued to shut me out emotionally. Before we married he'd been my best friend and confidant. But for years now he'd been emotionally absent and I missed him. I missed him when we sat in silence at the dinner table. I missed him when we slept in the same bed, a universe apart.

We weren't at the same place in our relationship with each other and we weren't at the same place in our spiritual walk. Jimmy didn't want to go to church as much as I did. He didn't want to read his Bible like I did. He didn't want to pray with me.

Loneliness was my constant companion. I wanted a husband I could talk to, one who would engage with me and be a spiritual leader in our family. I wanted our children to have a father who was really there for them. But he wasn't interested in filling those roles and balked if I even mentioned it.

When loneliness attempted to overwhelm me, I took solace in reading Jeremiah. Called the weeping prophet, Jeremiah might well have been the loneliest person on the pages of the Bible. Like me, he knew the strain of enduring long seasons of emotional isolation, so I comforted myself in reading what he said to God:

*Why is my pain perpetual*
*And my wound incurable,*
*Which refuses to be healed?*
*Will You surely be to me like an unreliable stream,*
*As waters that fail?* (Jeremiah 15:18, NKJV)

Although I realized that in some circumstances marital separation might be necessary, especially in situations of physical abuse, in my heart, I knew I couldn't leave Jimmy. And while I hated the pain, it was driving me toward God. I could have just coasted along if I hadn't been hurting so badly. But the pain made me so miserable it pushed me to keep changing and believing that by God's grace Jimmy, too, would eventually change.

He had to.

I couldn't live this way forever.

During those long years of loneliness, another Old Testament prophet I fell in love with was Habakkuk. He became a kind of spiritual chiropractor for me. When I was tempted to get stiff-necked and bent out of shape about the pressure I was under, he gave me an attitude adjustment. When I wanted to lash out in bitterness and complain, his words straightened me out.

I especially drew courage from the way Habakkuk handled the hard times in life. He said he'd rejoice in the Lord even if the worst happened.

*Though the fig tree may not blossom,*
*Nor fruit be on the vines;*
*Though the labor of the olive may fail,*
*And the fields yield no food;*
*Though the flock may be cut off from the fold,*
*And there be no herd in the stalls—*
*Yet I will rejoice in the Lord,*

*I will joy in the God of my salvation.*
*The Lord God is my strength;*
*He will make my feet like deer's feet,*
*And He will make me walk on my high hills.* (Habakkuk 3:16-19, NKJV)

"Lord," I prayed, "Even if Jimmy doesn't talk to me. Even if I'm lonely and suffer pain, I will rejoice and worship you all the days of my life."

When Jimmy raised his voice to me in anger, my heart said, *Even if...*

### A Pity Party Interrupted

One day in Bible study a woman shared her testimony and it sounded like she was telling my story. *What? I thought. Jimmy and I aren't the only ones going through this? Other people are struggling with the same things?*

Sure enough, it turned out that four or five women in my circle of friends were in a similar place in their marriages. Their husbands loved the Lord but acted like bullies toward them. We all needed help so we formed a little support group. We met together to talk about our problems and pray for our husbands.

I loved being with those women as we sought the Lord and prayed for one another. I was so happy and pumped when I got home one day that I didn't even blink when Jimmy yelled in my face.

It happened when I corrected Jimmy because he said something harsh to me. "Honey," I said, "you need to say that in love because love is patient and kind."

"Let me tell you something, Karen! Don't you *dare* use God's Word against me!"

I was so offended I promptly threw myself a pity party. But the

Lord interrupted it. He told me that Jimmy was right, and let me know that, to some degree, our little group had fallen into the trap of spiritual pride. One of the worst things we could do was to get all puffed up and use the Bible as a hammer to pound our husbands into shape. That would just spark more resentment in them and drive them farther away from us.

"Karen, don't ever use My Word to correct somebody," God said. "That's for Me to do and not you. You have no right to use it like that."

I was familiar enough with the voice of the Lord by then to know I'd heard Him clearly. So from that day forward I was careful not to repeat my mistake. Instead, I came up with a brand new one.

It happened when I started noticing that some of the Christian women I knew took the stronger, more dominant role in their marriage. If they were married to bullies, they acted like bullies too. I watched in awe at how these women took charge and spoke to their husbands in commanding tones. If not in words, at least in attitude their message was, "Get it together, Mister, and start treating me right! Pick up those clothes and start helping out around here! Take out the trash and *then* we'll see how I treat you!"

A few times I gathered my courage and tried this myself at home. That lasted about two seconds.

"You will *never* speak to me that way!" Jimmy said, enraged.

Once again, the Lord backed him. He revealed to me that although women are strong, the greatest gift we can give our husband is kindness and gentle humility.

As I studied what the Bible says about this, I found that, according to Proverbs 19:22, *kindness is what a man desires and that by treating Jimmy unkindly I could actually make it more difficult for him to change.* So I cried out to God according to the Scriptures. I prayed for kindness to be draped around me like a necklace, and said, *"Lord, make kindness the law of my tongue!"* (Prov. 3:3, 31:26).

I didn't experience an overnight transformation but the day came when I realized I was different. I no longer reacted to Jimmy's outbursts by running away and crying until there were no more tears.

While his words rained down on me like stones, my first thought was, *I've got to pray!*

Instead of crawling into an emotional hole, I quietly slipped away into my closet and cried out to God.

# CHAPTER SEVEN

*Toxic Thoughts and Wrong Words*

# 07

## Toxic Thoughts and Wrong Words

I woke early one morning after crying myself to sleep again. My eyes felt the size of soccer balls and my emotions felt like a throbbing mass of pain. It seemed as though Jimmy and I took one step forward and three steps back. Nobody on earth had the power to destroy me the way he did.

The same old thoughts circled my mind like a vulture circling a dying animal.

> *Nothing is ever going to change.*
> *It's always going to be this way.*
> *I deserve to be treated this way.*
> *God just needs to kill me.*

I picked up my Bible and opened it to where I'd been reading in Philippians, *"Finally, brothers and sisters, whatever is true, whatever is noble, whatever is right, whatever is pure, whatever is lovely, whatever is admirable—if anything is excellent or praiseworthy—think about such things."* (v. 8, NIV)

I'd read that verse many times before but this time it stopped me in my tracks. Remembering the thoughts I'd just entertained, I heard the Lord speak to me. "Karen," He said, "You're right. *Nothing is ever going to change*...until you change your thoughts! The way you've been thinking about yourself is not of Me."

All at once the puzzle pieces fell together in my mind. I'd been begging God to heal my insecurities for months, and He'd been telling me to change my thoughts. Maybe the two were connected!

Pondering the possibility I recalled what I'd read in 2 Corinthians 10:

> *For the weapons of our warfare are not carnal but mighty in God for pulling down strongholds, casting down arguments and every high thing that exalts itself against the knowledge of God, bringing every thought into captivity to the obedience of Christ.* (vv. 4-5, NIV)

Obviously, the devil was the enemy behind my insecurities; and according to those verses, taking my thoughts captive was a way to wage war against him. Therefore, this must be the secret to my emotional healing—casting down each and every one of my thoughts that dared to disagree with God!

The realization was, at once, both thrilling and overwhelming. For years I'd been controlled by devilish mental strongholds created by my negative thoughts and beliefs. Those thoughts and beliefs had been constructed out of the cruel and childish words my brother said to me as a child. They'd been built out of what Jimmy had said to me. They'd been based on the negative things other people had said about me.

They had not been established on what God had said about me.

None of my thoughts about myself were scriptural. I'd *never* thought good and noble and admirable things about myself!

For years I'd been so controlled through deceptive thoughts that I'd been blinded to the truth even when I saw it in the Bible. That's why I couldn't wrap my mind around Psalm 139:14, which says, *"I am fearfully and wonderfully made."* I couldn't see how it could possibly be talking about me. Although I wanted to believe it, the very idea was incomprehensible because my mind was fogged by the devil's lies.

Finally, I understood the root of my problems: My emotions were out of control because my thoughts were out of control. Toxic thoughts were bombarding me hundreds of times a day, making me feel depressed and hopeless.

But what in the world was I going to do about them?

I couldn't just ignore them. I had to replace them. So I started meditating on all the verses that dealt with thoughts. I camped for a while in Philippians, deliberately turning my attention toward things that were noble, right, pure, lovely and admirable. When I caught myself feeling depressed, I stopped to figure out what I'd been thinking and changed it.

## *Dealing with a Demon*

I was with a group of ladies from my church one day and they said, "Karen, you're so good at ministering to women. You always say great and helpful things."

Embarrassed, I wilted under their praise like a flower in the desert. "Are you kidding?" I asked. "I hate what I say. I hate who I am. I don't understand why you're saying anything nice about me."

Everyone went silent.

"What did you say?"

I repeated my sentiments.

"Karen, I think we've got to deal with a demon here."

"Okaaaay…" I said.

I knew that casting out demons is scriptural because the Bible says it's one of the signs that follow a believer. Personally, however, I didn't have any experience with it. Our church had a little deliverance program but it was new and we were still trying to find our way. So I felt a little skittish about getting involved.

Pushing aside my reluctance, I agreed to give it a try.

A few days later, my friends gathered around me in prayer and addressed the demonic forces that had been harassing me. During the process they asked, "What do you think?"

"I think you're all a joke," I said laughing.

"Yeah, that's a demon," one of them said.

I stifled another giggle and shrugged. "Whatever!"

When they finished praying for me I didn't feel any different; but they were confident their purpose had been accomplished.

"You'll notice after this that your thinking has changed," they said. "When circumstances come up, you'll process them in a different way and that will be a sign to you that something really happened."

The next day I was ironing and a woman called who always intimidated and upset me. She pulled her usual manipulation and control tactics, but for the first time, I didn't react. I processed the experience differently than I ever had before!

In the days following, it seemed as though the Word flooded into me in a deeper way and I began to grow in the Lord. It was as though I experienced spiritual growth on steroids. In short order, I completely outgrew that friend's manipulative tactics.

When she couldn't control me anymore it upset her. She got her confidence from being needed by other people and she hated to see me confident and strong. But the hole in my soul was healing and I was no longer desperate for her approval.

Although deliverance didn't change the fact that I had to continue taking my thoughts captive, it helped the process along.

## Taking a Page from David's Playbook

While the Lord was teaching me to retrain my thoughts, He also started dealing with me about my words. One day I read Ecclesiastes 5:2: *"Do not be rash with your mouth, and let not your heart utter anything hastily before God. For God is in heaven, and you on earth; therefore let your words be few"* (NKJV). Instantly convicted, I slapped my hand over my mouth. I'd not only allowed myself to think in opposition to God's Word, I'd also spoken in opposition to Him!

I remembered David's self-talk that's recorded in Psalms, which I'd grown to love. He said:

> *As the deer pants for streams of water,*
> *so my soul pants for you, my God.*
> *My soul thirsts for God, for the living God.*
> *When can I go and meet with God?*
> *My tears have been my food*
> *day and night,*
> *while people say to me all day long,*
> *"Where is your God?"* (Ps. 42:1-3, NIV)

David often started out telling God how troubled he was about what was happening in his life, but he never stayed in the place of complaint. He always changed his tune and started encouraging himself.

> *Why, my soul, are you downcast?*
> *Why so disturbed within me?*
> *Put your hope in God,*
> *for I will yet praise him,*
> *my Savior and my God.*

> *My soul is downcast within me;*
>   *therefore I will remember you*
> *from the land of the Jordan,*
>   *the heights of Hermon—from Mount Mizar.*
>   *Deep calls to deep*
>   *in the roar of your waterfalls;*
>   *all your waves and breakers*
>   *have swept over me.*
>   *By day the Lord directs his love,*
>   *at night his song is with me—*
>   *a prayer to the God of my life.* (v. 5-8, NIV)

As I meditated on those scriptures I came to a decision. If David could say such things by faith, so could I. I turned to Psalm 139:14 and confessed, "Father, I praise you because I am fearfully and wonderfully made."

Saying those words almost made me feel faint, but I reminded myself it was only because I'd believed a lie and the enemy had used it to build a stronghold in my mind.

## A Whole New Kind of Pregnant

Demolishing such strongholds, I realized, was going to be an uphill battle for me—at least for a while. I'd spent most of my life putting more confidence in how I felt about myself and my situation than I did in what God said. I'd lived for years letting my thoughts and feelings whip me around like the wind and waves.

Although I'd prayed countless prayers asking God to heal me, I'd almost always done it without faith. As a result my life was a perfect picture of James 1:6:

> *Only it must be in faith that he asks with no wavering (no hesitating, no doubting). For the one who wavers (hesitates, doubts) is like the billowing surge out at sea that is blown hither and thither and tossed by the wind.* (AMP)

I'd never really understood before that faith isn't based on feelings or what's visible to the natural eye; that it's something invisible we have on the inside. But, at last, I was catching on. I started thinking of having faith as kind of like being pregnant. When I was first pregnant with my children, no one could tell it by looking at me. Yet a seed in me had been fertilized and was growing. It was being fed, oblivious to what was happening in the outside world.

That's what was happening to me spiritually as I believed God's Word. I didn't feel any different. I didn't look any different. I still had to battle to control my thoughts. But the seed of what God said about me had been fertilized and had taken root in me. He was healing me from the inside out.

To experience the full manifestation of my miracle, I had to keep feeding on God's Word. I had to continue to believe that what He said was true even before I could see any evidence of it.

One thing that helped me do this was the paradigm shift I'd made: I no longer thought everything was all about me. It was all about God, and faith is very important to Him. As Hebrews 11:6 says, *"Without faith it is impossible to please Him, for he who comes to God must believe that He is, and that He is a rewarder of those who diligently seek Him"* (NIV). To me this meant, instead of being afraid of God, I had to continually trust His Word and believe He would reward me for it.

Such faith, simple as it sounds, didn't come easy to me. I was used to being tossed around by my thoughts and feelings, and I didn't wake up one morning stable as a rock. It was a process; a long, slow journey. Every time I meditated on God's Word I took another tiny step forward.

Every time I believed what He said I changed a little.

God's Word truly is *alive*. It's sharper than a two-edged sword. So the more I read it, the more it cut away my old, damaged way of thinking. The more it renewed my mind in accordance with His original blueprint.

## *One Thought at a Time*

Spending time daily in God's Word helped me think praiseworthy, thankful thoughts, but turning those thoughts into words seemed to be a real challenge for me. I felt thankful, but I had trouble getting myself to say it. So I asked the Lord to help me think about Jesus all the time. "Lord," I prayed, "let me go to sleep thinking about You and wake up thinking about You."

I disciplined myself every night to pray, "Lord, thank You for being with me. Thank You for loving me today. I love You Father. I love You Jesus."

Then I went to sleep.

When I woke the next morning my first thought was, *You're on my mind!* So I made myself say, "Lord, I'm so thankful that you answered my prayer and you're on my mind this morning!"

That's how I started: one thought and one word at a time.

When I found myself worrying, I stopped myself and said, "Thank you, Lord that you've taken this worry for me. You carry all my burdens and I don't have to carry it." Then I knelt down and worshiped and praised God, confessing His Word.

I discovered that praise, worship and thanksgiving not only changed my thought process, it worked like a nuclear blast against the enemy. It blew him out of my way and ushered me straight into the presence of God.

As the months passed and I continued to struggle to believe God loved me, I meditated on scriptures about love in Song of Solomon and Psalms. I pictured the Lord speaking those verses directly to me. I imagined Him cherishing me like a bridegroom cherishes a bride, and read:

> *Daughters of kings are among your honored women;*
> *at your right hand is the royal bride in gold of Ophir.*
> *Listen, daughter, and pay careful attention:*
> *Forget your people and your father's house.*
> *Let the king be enthralled by your beauty;*
> *honor him, for he is your lord.*
> *The city of Tyre will come with a gift,*
> *people of wealth will seek your favor.*
> *All glorious is the princess within her chamber;*
> *her gown is interwoven with gold.*
> *In embroidered garments she is led to the king;*
> *her virgin companions follow her—*
> *those brought to be with her.*
> *Led in with joy and gladness,*
> *they enter the palace of the king.* (Psalm 45:9-15, NIV)

That psalm became a signpost of hope for me. It was an assurance that while the fire hurt, I was in the process of being refined like gold. In my mind, Jesus desired me and longed to give me my every desire.

The most staggering thing was that it was *true*.

# CHAPTER EIGHT

*A Woman and a Well*

# 08

*A Woman and a Well*

I braced my foot against the floorboard and put my hand on the dash, almost breaking out into a cold sweat. Jimmy had zoned out, oblivious to the traffic and what was going on around him. "Slow down!" I said. "Turn here!"

"Don't start on me!" he hissed, clenching his jaw. "I don't need you telling me how to drive!"

*Here we go*, I thought.

My stomach tied itself into a knot and my heart fluttered in my chest like a captive butterfly. Jimmy's anger charged the air like lighting before a storm, electrifying the atmosphere in the car until I almost felt my hair floating up and standing on end. I knew how this trip would turn out if I yielded to my knee-jerk reaction; and for months I'd sensed the Lord urging me to respond in a different way when I was confronted with these first fiery flashes of a fight. Clearly, He expected me to change my behavior regardless of how Jimmy chose to act.

But what could I do?

As I tried to think despite the adrenalin rushing through my body, six words flitted through my mind.

*The truth will set you free.*

My breath hitched as I remembered a truth about myself God had recently revealed to me. Telling Jimmy about it would mean lowering my emotional walls. I shuddered at the thought, wondering if it wouldn't be safer to fight.

Was I really ready for this kind of vulnerability?

Without taking time to answer that question, I plunged in like a kid off the high dive.

"I think I have a fear of dying."

"What?" Jimmy asked.

I cleared my throat and said, "I think I'm afraid of a car wreck."

He took his eyes off the road and blinked at me.

"When you drive that way…"

"Don't start on me! I didn't do anything!"

"I know! I know! Just let me say something."

"Okay."

"I'm not saying you're doing anything wrong. It's me. I've finally figured out that I'm afraid of dying in a car wreck and when you drive a certain way, I feel afraid."

"But I didn't…" he said, his hackles rising.

"I'm not saying you did anything wrong."

"A car wreck, huh? How long has that been going on?"

"I'm not sure, but I've had nightmares about dying in a car wreck for years. It's odd, really. I have nightmares about tornadoes but I never die in them, so I'm not afraid of tornadoes. I'm not afraid of flying. I'm not afraid of heights. I'm not even afraid of snakes. But I am afraid of a car wrecks, so I think when we get in the car I feel out of control and I get scared."

"That's why you nag at me?"

"Yeah, I guess that's why I start bracing myself and telling you how to drive."

"I don't like it when you criticize my driving, Karen."

"I realize that, but I'm hoping if you know I'm afraid it will help you understand and maybe you won't react. I'm trying to figure out how to diffuse these car fights."

## One Small Victory

"Okay," he said, processing.

"You know honey, sometimes when you're behind the wheel I don't feel like you're paying attention."

"But I *am* paying attention!" he said, frustrated.

"I'm talking about how I feel here, so can we just focus on that for a minute?"

He took a deep breath and let it out on a sigh. "Sure."

"When I feel like you're not paying attention, I get scared."

"Now wait a minute!"

"Jimmy," I said, struggling to stay calm while still bracing myself against the dash, "I want to explain how I feel."

"Okay, but make it quick because I don't want to be late."

"I feel as though getting where we're going matters more to you than the fact that I'm afraid."

"Oh," he said with a spark of understanding in his eyes. He looked at the traffic and glanced at the speedometer. Then he took his foot off the accelerator and slowed down.

I breathed a deep sigh of relief. We spent the rest of the trip in silence, each of us pondering my revelation. We reached our destination without a fight. When we got out of the car, Jimmy took my arm with a tenderness he hadn't expressed in a long time.

That small victory felt empowering.

## Exposing Satan's Lies

*If only I could think of a way to diffuse all our fights. That would be marvelous!*

I wondered if such a thing might actually be possible. Maybe it would if I understood more clearly what the real problem was.

As I searched God's Word for answers, I noticed a common theme that pointed me toward the solution I'd been seeking. It was a theme I found all through Bible, but what Jesus said about it in Matthew 22:35-40 especially caught my attention. There, a Pharisee asked Him to identify the greatest commandment in the law and Jesus answered by saying:

> *'Love the Lord your God with all your heart and with all your soul and with all your mind.' This is the first and greatest commandment. And the second is like it: 'Love your neighbor as yourself.' All the Law and the Prophets hang on these two commandments.* (NIV)

*Everything* in God's kingdom, it seemed, hinged on love; everything, including all the law, boiled down to love.

This made perfect sense to me. My deepest longing had always been to love and be loved. It's what I craved above all else. I'd never been a woman who needed a fancy house or beautiful clothes. My heart's cry had always been: *Just love me! Please love me!*

Like most little girls, I grew up believing that heart cry would be answered if I just married the perfect man and had a great marriage. So I'd always assumed my unhappy marriage was the cause of my pain. Thinking that if only Jimmy loved me I'd be peaceful and happy, I'd done everything I could to earn his love. When I failed I'd concluded I was simply unlovable.

But the whole thing had been a deception.

According to 1 John 4:10, *"In this is love, not that we loved God, but that He loved us and sent His Son to be the propitiation for our sins."* Jesus had already provided for me the love I'd been craving. He'd loved me always—even when I didn't deserve it. But instead of looking to Him for love, I'd looked to other sources. When they failed me, I'd swallowed even more of Satan's lies.

"Your husband doesn't love you because you're worthless," the enemy whispered.

"Nobody else feels like you do."

"You're all alone."

"You should never have married him."

## *Drinking from the Wrong Well*

Like the woman at the well in the fourth chapter of John, I'd tried to drink the wrong water—the kind that couldn't satisfy my thirst. I'd tried, as a child, to draw the love I needed from my parents' well. When I became a wife, I'd tried to get it from Jimmy's well. I'd tried to drink from my friends' wells. But now the truth was beginning to dawn on me.

No man, no marriage, nothing on earth could ever fill the emptiness I felt inside. Only God could give me that kind of love. It wasn't available from anyone else.

As I studied the Bible, I saw a glimmer of the truth: Jimmy's love—even if he poured it out on me like a flood—would never be enough for me because my heart had been pierced through by the arrows of Satan's lies. It leaked like a sieve! For me to be whole, to be able to give and receive love the way God intended, the wounds in my heart had to be healed. And the only medicine powerful enough to heal them was a revelation of God's love.

I'd heard stories of people who got saved and were changed in the twinkling of an eye; some were delivered from addictions and never wanted drugs or alcohol again; others were instantly set free from anger or fear. Those testimonies thrilled me, but I didn't have that kind of experience. I wasn't transformed overnight because someone laid their hands on me and prayed. Although deliverance helped, it didn't dramatically alter me.

Nothing in my life came quick and easy. For me, the changes emerged like slow-growing seeds. They appeared like tiny buds here and there, and unfurled in almost imperceptible increments, week by week and month by month, as I kept my heart turned toward the light of God's Word.

Although everything about the process took longer than I wanted, eventually, Jimmy saw the way I'd changed. It was impossible to miss.

I hoped he'd be so thrilled that he'd wrap me in his arms and apologize for all the hateful things he'd said. But that didn't happen. He just took the kindness and honor I gave him as if it were his due, and kept treating me the same old way.

## *The Voice of the Accuser*

One evening when I felt like I'd been stretched to the limit, I almost bit off my tongue trying to keep from snapping back at him as another fight erupted. I was exhausted with the effort it took to keep the peace. Instead of restraining myself, I wanted to take the dinner I'd prepared for him and pour over his head like I'd done that time when we were dating.

I felt like I was being stoned as he pelted me with words that cut and bruised me. His was the voice of the accuser, blaming and accusing me of being the source of all our problems.

*I'd read in the Bible about Joshua standing before the High Priest being accused by Satan (Zech. 3:2). I'd read about the trouble Job suffered at the hands of the same Accuser* (Job 1:6). In my mind, I knew the enemy those two Old Testament saints had encountered was behind the trouble in my life, too. But in my emotions I felt like Jimmy was the villain.

*Who expects the people closest to you will be the ones to give voice to the devil's accusations?* I wondered. *Who expects them to be the ones who hurt you the most?*

I apologized just to stop the argument, but resentment rose like bile in my throat. I wanted to give up. To lash out. To run away. Anything to make the pain stop.

When I could get alone with God I registered all my complaints with Him. "No matter how nice I am, he refuses to change!"

In response, God reminded me of a lesson I thought I'd already learned. "Karen," He said, "instead of *living* the Word, you're just trying to use it to change your situation."

"What?"

"Who are you living for? Who are you trying to please? If your goal is to let Christ be expressed through you, why would Jimmy not changing make you want to give up?"

I pondered those words as they pricked and deflated my own self-satisfied pride.

"My motive for treating Jimmy well should not be just to get my way."

"Right."

This, I realized, was one of the secret mysteries of God's kingdom. His way is the exact opposite of the way of the world and the flesh. The greatest enemy in my life wasn't the way Jimmy treated me.

The greatest enemy I faced was my flesh, my mind, and my own human reasoning.

I'd always thought that if my circumstances were different…if only Jimmy treated me the way I deserved…if only I weren't so shy and insecure…I'd be an amazing, awesome Christian. But in reality those were the very things God was using to uncover the areas where

I needed to change and grow. He expected me to be the Christian He'd called me to be now, regardless of what Jimmy did or didn't do.

This was a big pill for me to swallow, especially in light of the role Jimmy had been given at church. He was actually teaching the Life Group we'd been asked to lead! What's more, the group was growing and multiplying at an amazing rate. Many of the members were single and we were helping them with relationship issues. Yet all the while we still had some struggles in our own marriage.

At the time, this baffled me. How could Jimmy impart God's wisdom to others and not be living it fully himself? In hindsight, I can see the answer is simple: While I read the Word so that God could change me; Jimmy read it so he could understand it and teach.

As a result, fights continued to erupt if I didn't agree with everything he said, as soon as he said it.

"You just don't talk to me right!" he railed, one night after he came home late.

I kissed his cheek and reheated his dinner. "I know you're stressed, but the kids and I need you too."

He ratcheted his volume up a few degrees. "I spend all day out fighting battles and all you do is complain!"

As time passed and the tension between us kept mounting, I endeavored to keep my temper in check. I didn't slam doors. I didn't cry. I didn't run out of the house and drive around. I treated him with kindness and respect.

But in the midst of it all, one thing did happen that neither Jimmy nor I had expected. The more I fed on God's Word, the more my heart healed and the more I realized I didn't have to put up with his bad behavior.

Up to this point, he'd always been able to verbally abuse me until I would cave in and agree with him. But now I would no longer bow down to him or let him to destroy me…which meant he no longer had me under his control.

## Symptoms of a Sick Marriage

When he found a small isolated rash had cropped up on his skin, neither of us was very concerned. But when it spread, he called and made an appointment with a dermatologist. The doctor stripped him down to his shorts and did an examination. After finishing the doctor said, "Get dressed. The nurse will be back in a few minutes with some information for you."

A few minutes later, the nurse returned with a tape recorder. "The doctor wants you to listen to this tape," she explained.

The audio tape explained the damage that unchecked stress and worry could cause the body. It listed such things as high blood pressure, hair loss, Irritable Bowel Syndrome, lower back pain, skin disease and outbreaks of rashes. Embarrassed that the doctor had seen through his tough guy exterior and diagnosed the real problem, Jimmy sat in the exam room overwhelmed that our fractured marriage and his exhausting workload had caused him to become physically sick.

When the tape ended, Jimmy left the office like a man on death row walking to the electric chair. Something that had been walled off in him for years cracked open. By the time he reached his car tears streamed down his face. He hadn't cried since the night he repented and begged me to marry him, but once the tears started, he couldn't get them to stop.

It was as if a deep well of grief and regret had opened up within him. How had he let things come to this? Emotionally raw and vulnerable, he experienced a strange awakening. He realized that for years he'd been simmering with anger, stress, arrogance, and resentment—all of which had been fueled by his own insecurity. That insecurity had driven him to keep a tight, dominating grip on everything around him—including his wife. Now his grip was beginning to slip.

He had no idea what to do about it.

# CHAPTER NINE

*The Perfect Storm*

# 09
## The Perfect Storm

I had no idea that Jimmy had wept and cried out to God for help after seeing the dermatologist. But it was the crack in the dike that started a trickle that became a flood. Jimmy began to be more emotionally open to me than ever before. It was like the tape he had listened to at the doctor's office touched something in him that had never been touched before.

Jimmy hated weakness. It was ingrained in him from childhood that the Evans' couldn't be weak. And now he was having to come to terms with the reality that his skin problems were a glaring announcement that he wasn't the man he thought he was. And that included his role as a husband.

In all of our married lives there had only been a few times Jimmy had ever shown any weakness. The first was after three years of marriage when I confronted Jimmy about playing too much golf. He yelled at me and told me to get out of the house and go back to my parents. Before then Jimmy had been completely checked-out and was either working or playing golf.

He had little to do with the kids or me and I had finally had enough. I had prayed hard that Jimmy would change but nothing happened.

But on the night I confronted him and he told me to get out something changed. As I was crying in the bedroom the Lord was breaking through Jimmy's heart in the living room.

Jimmy describes it as scales falling from his eyes and for the first time he could see how much of a jerk he was. To my amazement he came in the bedroom and for the first time he said he was sorry. He also told me he was hanging up his golf clubs.

That was something I never expected to hear.

Jimmy followed through with his promise and that was the beginning of a healing work that took place in our marriage. Even though our problems didn't end there by any means, it stopped a terrible season in our marriage that would have surely ended in divorce if the Lord would not have come through.

Now, Jimmy was showing weakness again. It was endearing to me because I've always told him that humility is attractive. But even though he was becoming more open about his emotions he was also dealing with a lot of stress from his parents and work. This caused him to be very volatile over the next few months.

One night when Jimmy came home from work exhausted we got into a huge fight. Jimmy yelled at me and told me I was rebellious. When I heard those words I became furious. I stomped into the bedroom and I was too mad to cry. I just sat on my bed and prayed and asked the Lord to give me the strength to endure being married to such a difficult man.

Even though I had surrendered many times before I wasn't going to do it this time. There was a new strength in me that was from the Lord. I wanted to be a good wife but I wasn't going to lie just to make Jimmy happy. I wasn't rebellious. Jimmy was a controlling chauvinist who had to have everything his way. He was better than earlier in our marriage but this fight was proof that the old Jimmy was still alive.

But then something surprising happened. As I sat in the bedroom praying the door opened and Jimmy walked in. As he walked toward me on the bed I could tell something was different. And was it ever!

Jimmy sat down on the bed next to me and said, "Karen, I'm so sorry for the way I have acted. I have been terrible to you and I am so sorry. You have done nothing wrong and I am the problem. I will do anything necessary to change. I am so sorry for the hurtful words I've spoken to you and I will never do it again. I love you with all of my heart and you mean more to me than anything else. I will quit my job or do anything else necessary to change and be the husband I need to be."

That was the night the old Jimmy died and the man I had prayed for appeared. He was totally sincere and when he woke up the next morning he was a new man with a completely different attitude.

## A Time to Build

Everything that happens in a marriage—good or bad—affects both people. So when Jimmy repented, it not only affected him, it affected me as well. I felt as though someone had unlocked the door and I'd been let out of an emotional prison.

"The first thing we're going to do," Jimmy said, "is schedule time to talk."

Oddly enough, I initially felt almost allergic to the idea. For years our talks had only resulted in my feeling beat down and destroyed. I'd missed the closeness we used to have but I wasn't eager to sign up for another round of verbal smack-down. He insisted, though, and I knew we had to trust one another enough to start somewhere.

From the outset I set some ground rules for myself. I knew if our emotional walls were going to come down there were some things I couldn't do. While I would be honest with him, I couldn't beat him up for all the things he'd done wrong for years. It would never work if I judged and condemned him. No matter how tempting it may have been, I would not mother him.

I put those constraints on myself because I knew that was what God expected of me. Jimmy had asked for forgiveness. My part was to forgive and not punish him.

Although my flesh wanted to make him pay, if I did it I knew that I'd miss out on the joy of sharing his deepest feelings with him. With that as my goal, I figured the potential payoff was well worth the price.

Jimmy scheduled time for us to talk the next evening. Although we wanted to be alone, we'd never let our kids watch TV unless we were in the room. They weren't used to sitting by themselves and watching shows. So we read them bedtime stories and put them to bed early. Then we popped popcorn and went to the little sitting room off our bedroom. Jimmy could tell I was leery; his idea of talking usually involved lectures, sex, or both.

## *Simple Communication: No Sex Required*

"We're going to sit here and talk," Jimmy said. "And I promise, we don't even have to have sex."

"Seriously?" I asked, shocked. If he pulled that off I'd be impressed.

We sat down and talked like we had in high school. With no sex involved. He said, "You know, I want to be married right." I loved hearing that; it was a balm to my heart. Curling up in my chair, I enjoyed every moment as a seemingly new version of my husband told me even the most trivial things about his day at the appliance store. Astonished, I realized he really did just want to talk.

The second time it happened I felt a reconnection with him, and for the first time in years I was able to let down my guard.

The third night we talked, I just about jumped the boy's bones. He was stunned at my response because men don't get it. They don't realize how much they can gain by being open and communicating with us. They don't grasp the power behind that.

God created women to talk. Even from a developmental point of view, little girls talk before little boys do. No wonder a woman was the first person Satan tried to engage in conversation! We love to talk. Why? Because we love the emotional connection it creates.

As my conversations with Jimmy continued, I noticed another big change in him. He started helping around the house. This was unheard of. The first time I saw him vacuuming the carpet I thought I was hallucinating. When I asked him about it, he confided that he'd always been hesitant to help for fear that he would become the male maid.

Hearing him admit to any kind of fear surprised me. He'd always been such a strong, dominant man that I'd never thought about him feeling afraid. As we worked through some of our issues, however, we realized we'd both been reacting out of different kinds of fear.

Eventually Jimmy acknowledged it was the fear factor that had caused him to wall himself off from me. He'd been unwilling to let down his emotional guard down for fear of being controlled. That's why it was hard for him to express any form of weakness. If his feelings were hurt, he stuffed them rather than being honest about them because he didn't want to reveal his vulnerabilities and run the risk of me taking advantage of them.

Only after months of talking through our emotional issues did I realize that when Jimmy attacked me verbally, it was his way of saying, "That hurts my feelings!"

Sometimes just the look on my face hurt him, he explained. Other times my tone of voice or my complaints—no matter how necessary or honest—hurt him. For five long years of marriage and four years of dating I'd never figured that out.

I knew that when I was stressed, exhausted or at the end of my emotional rope, the tone of my voice changed. But a lot of times that had nothing to do with Jimmy at all. I was reacting to something else entirely. But he always took it personally. Even if it didn't have anything to do with him, when I frowned or sounded irritated he felt attacked.

One day after we'd been doing well for quite a while, I was exhausted and said something with a harsh tone and it produced the same results. "You're not going to get away with talking to me that way!" he snapped.

I took a deep breath and thought, *This isn't who we are any more. This isn't the way we act. It's nothing more than a wrong behavior.*

"Wait!" I said, "I'm sorry I said it that way. I know better." With that response, the argument dissipated before it began.

In addition to making sure we spent time talking after the kids were in bed, Jimmy scheduled date nights for us and he was careful not to let them get canceled because something else came up. Date nights once a week became one of the Ten Commandments of our married life. We put our relationship ahead of our children, because if we weren't healthy, the family couldn't be healthy. Over the years we'd seen so many cases of couples, especially those who'd battled infertility, lose their relationship because they made their children their focus. We never let our children take the place of our marriage.

## *A Relational Roller Coaster Ride*

We also realized that we each came into the marriage with conscious and subconscious ways of handling issues in life based on what worked for our parents. For the first time in our marriage, we sat down and discussed in depth what boundaries we wanted for our own family. This included everything from how we wanted to handle holidays to how we would raise our children.

One of the biggest issues we had to deal with was our different perspectives on handling money. Jimmy was a spender and I was a saver. After fighting for years about which one of us was right, we finally talked it through and found a compromise. I told Jimmy, "I don't care if you spend, so long as we have money going regularly into savings." Watching our savings grow gave me a feeling of great satisfaction and eliminated another point of conflict that had once triggered fights.

While all of this resulted in some wonderful new changes in our relationship, I don't want to imply that just because Jimmy repented and we started following a set of principles that everything just worked out. That's not how it went. For a while it was a non-stop roller coaster ride.

One minute everything was lovey-dovey and we were looking at one another with cow eyes. The next thing *Wham!* out of nowhere the fight was on. Some hidden issue, like a fast-moving current that had been swept under the rug, would knock our feet out from under us and drag us right back where we'd been six months earlier.

There was nothing neat and tidy about it. We had great moments… and bad moments. We experienced great episodes…and awful episodes. There were more great moments…more great moments…more great moments…and then one of the worst episodes we'd ever known.

Sometimes the fall from awesome to awful was so hard and so harsh that it felt like madness. *How could one petty little thing throw us back into spitting nails at one another?* I'd wonder.

I finally realized I had to accept the fact that it was going to take time to undo years of bad behavior, miscommunication and dysfunction. The key was to keep trying, to keep working on it, to continue talking, to try and understand one another.

## *Out of the Ashes Grows the Sweetest Fruit*

Dinner simmered on the stove while I put dishes on the table waiting for Jimmy to get home. As I pondered our situation, I realized that we'd been rocking along well for over a month without any major fights or hurt feelings. Then out of nowhere, one of the kids pulled something and I found myself standing on Jimmy's last nerve, and he on mine. I discovered that physical exhaustion, high stress levels and hectic, too-tight schedules triggered those old responses. With a huge sigh we each realized that we had to go back and work through things again. We had to deal with it *again*. We had to get past it *again*.

No, it wasn't fun, but what was the alternative? Going back to living in a war zone? Refusing to speak to each other? Getting a divorce? None of those were an option so we just picked ourselves up and went to work putting things back together. We learned to be quick to accept responsibility for what we did and quick to repent.

It was hard work but what we reaped was a harvest of passion.

It wouldn't be fair to say that we got our marriage back, because what we were building with each other had never existed. Rather than "falling back in love," for the first time in our marriage we were experiencing deep intimacy. It was sexual, yes, but it went deeper than that.

We were establishing an emotional connection that wasn't based on dysfunction and neediness. Our emotional barriers fell like the walls of Jericho and from the ruins of that destruction grew the sweetest fruit.

It didn't happen overnight, but over time we went from the pinnacle of pain to powerful passion. That's when I realized I finally had what I'd always wanted: A wonderful relationship with the two great loves of my life.

Each morning I run to the first one—into the arms of Jesus where I am healed, restored, strengthened and loved. Each night I fall into Jimmy's arms and offer him the fruit of what Jesus has done for me: love, joy, peace, forbearance, kindness, goodness, faithfulness, gentleness and self-control.

I know beyond a doubt that if I hadn't found what I needed in Jesus I would never have experienced what I have with Jimmy. I owe both my life and my marriage to Him.

# CHAPTER TEN

*The Time to Change*

# 10

## *The Time to Change*

"Karen, I need some advice," a woman from church said when I answered the telephone. "My marriage is falling apart and I just don't know what to do."

You're asking *me?* I thought.

It seemed no matter how many calls like this I received, they always surprised me. After everything Jimmy and I had been through, I still found it amazing that anyone would want marital advice from me.

With the phone pressed against my ear, I settled into a comfortable chair and listened as yet another wife sobbed out her story. So much of it sounded familiar. I knew exactly what she was feeling as she described what it had been like for her as she tried to navigate her way through the minefield that had become her marriage.

"I don't think I can do this anymore," she said, her voice tense with exasperation. "He knows what he needs to do but he just won't change! He's just so…"

I stopped her in mid-sentence.

"Listen to me," I said. "If you don't hear another word, I want you to pay close attention to this."

"Okay."

"He doesn't get it! I promise you, he doesn't get it. Men are not wired like we are. They process things differently than we do. They're more compartmentalized. You can describe to your husband in detail how his behavior is hurting you and he may shake his head as though he understands, but trust me, he doesn't get it. Intelligence has nothing to do with it. Jimmy is smart but he didn't get it for five years."

"But our problems seem so obvious!" she said. "Why can't he see them?"

"Do you remember in the Bible where it says that we can't fight spiritual wars with carnal weapons?"

"Yeah."

"This is one of those situations. The mess you're dealing with isn't just a tangle of natural problems. There's a spiritual component involved. The devil is working to blind your eyes and your husband's to the truth that can set you free. You can't argue away those spiritual blinders. You can't shout and make him understand. To make your marriage work, you have to do what's needed in the natural and you also have to do spiritual warfare."

She sniffed and blew her nose. "I don't know where to start."

"That part's easy," I said, "you have to start with you."

## A Work in Progress

After we finished our conversation, I put down the phone and felt a cloud of insecurity overshadow me. Condemning thoughts poured from it like rain. *Who are you to be giving her counsel? You've got no right to open your mouth! Look at your own marriage!*

It was true; Jimmy and I were still a work in progress. Although we were being bombarded by Christian couples asking us for help, we were still in the process of putting our own marriage back together.

And sometimes it seemed as though we still had a long way to go.

Yes, Jimmy and I were leagues better than we'd been before, our relationship was continuing to heal and grow, and I loved rehearsing what God had done for us…but was I really qualified to talk to the women who called me for advice? I wondered.

One day I was reading the Bible and the Lord brought this passage to my attention:

> *Then those who feared the Lord talked with each other, and the Lord listened and heard. A scroll of remembrance was written in his presence concerning those who feared the Lord and honored his name.*
>
> *"On the day when I act," says the Lord Almighty, "they will be my treasured possession. I will spare them, just as a father has compassion and spares his son who serves him. And you will again see the distinction between the righteous and the wicked, between those who serve God and those who do not.* (Mal. 3:16-18, NIV)

Those verses answered my question. When I talked to others about what God had done for Jimmy and me, the Lord was recording what I said in a scroll of remembrance. I *loved* that! It meant He was pleased with those conversations.

Qualified or not, I didn't have to wait until my marriage was picture perfect to share what God had taught me. He didn't want me to wait. He wanted to speak now to these hurting people—and He needed a voice.

I smiled and remembered Isaiah.

*Here am I, Lord. Send me.*

## A New Role

Over the next few years as Jimmy and I continued to work on our marriage, our Life Group kept expanding, and increasing numbers of people began asking us for marital help. Our pastor saw what was happening and asked Jimmy to come on staff.

At first, he didn't feel he could accept the offer. "There's no way you can afford to pay me what I'm making now," he explained. "And I can't afford to quit my job."

"Well, pray about it," the pastor said.

Jimmy had known for years he was called to ministry but he always thought he should get some formal training first. A couple of years earlier when he'd tried to make that work, though, he'd hit a dead end. So he just continued to lead our Life Group and work at his parents' appliance store.

When our pastor called the second time, he had good news. "I think we can pay you more now."

Jimmy accepted the position he was offered and joined the church staff as a pre-marriage and marriage counselor. He was wonderful at his job and helped many people. In addition to counseling, when our pastor was out of town, he filled the pulpit.

After ten months on staff Jimmy was approached by the elders of the church. The senior pastor had resigned and was taking a church in Florida and they wanted him to fill that role. He agreed and, at 29 years old, he became the senior pastor.

On April 30, 1994, I was asked to lead the church's women's ministries. I didn't feel confident in my ability to do it, but I accepted the position anyway. Although I wasn't a teacher or a preacher, I took solace in knowing I could share with other women what God had done in my life. Stepping out by faith on God's word, I looked for guidance to Philippians 2:

*Therefore if you have any encouragement from being united with Christ, if any comfort from his love, if any common sharing in the Spirit, if any tenderness and compassion, then make my joy complete by being like-minded, having the same love, being one in spirit and of one mind. Do nothing out of selfish ambition or vain conceit. Rather, in humility value others above yourselves, not looking to your own interests but each of you to the interests of the others.*

*In your relationships with one another, have the same mindset as Christ Jesus: Who, being in very nature God, did not consider equality with God something to be used to his own advantage; rather, he made himself nothing by taking the very nature of a servant, being made in human likeness. And being found in appearance as a man, he humbled himself by becoming obedient to death—even death on a cross!*

*Therefore God exalted him to the highest place and gave him the name that is above every name, that at the name of Jesus every knee should bow, in heaven and on earth and under the earth, and every tongue acknowledge that Jesus Christ is Lord, to the glory of God the Father.* (v. 1-11, NIV)

I'd found in my own life that knowing Jesus is everything and that we as believers must first and foremost find our identity in Him. So I thought the simplest way to help the women at the church would be to emphasize the importance of their spending time with the Lord and to encourage them to get to know Him.

*This will be easy,* I thought. *It's so basic!*

Basic or not, however, I soon made a startling discovery. Most of our ladies knew next to nothing about having a real relationship with God. As a result, they didn't really know Jesus on a personal level. Even some of the elders' wives, confided in me, "We've never had a

quiet time. We don't read the Bible."
*Alright then,* I thought, *we'll start at the very beginning.*

## A Few Things We've Learned

As I write this book almost forty years have passed since that landmark day when God broke through Jimmy's heart and started changing him. During those years he and I have not only walked out the healing of our own marriage, we've counseled countless others whose marriages were in crisis. In the process, we've learned some things that I feel are important for me to mention.

First of all, we've come to understand that, while our goal is to help people save their marriages, there are some situations that should not be tolerated. For instance, there is no excuse for abuse. No one should stay in a situation where they or their children are being physically, emotionally or sexually abused. There are also situations of adultery and abandonment that can end a marriage in spite of the efforts of a righteous spouse.

And serious substance abuse or other addictions can also create unlivable circumstances if they aren't dealt with seriously.

Clearly, such situations are serious. They pose unique hazards that must be specifically addressed.

Otherwise, however, we've learned that most couples face pretty much the same marital issues. To a greater or lesser degree, we all have to deal with things like communication, finances, sex, fleshly behaviors, anger, bitterness, and unforgiveness.

And every marriage, no matter how good, needs work to stay healthy.

## *Deadly Mindsets*

One form of toxic thinking I've found to be very common in women with unhappy marriages is unforgiveness. They often let the hurts inflicted on them by their husbands fester and turn into offense. Eventually the offense hardens into bitterness.

Sometimes, even when I show them in the Bible that they need to let the offense go and forgive, they refuse to do it. That always scares me because I know they don't grasp the danger they're putting themselves in. The Word of God says anyone who doesn't forgive will be turned over to tormentors. The torment of bitterness is like cancer of the soul. It's deadly.

Another mindset I've found that can be deadly in a marriage is a judgmental attitude. I see that all the time. Women who don't like the way their husbands are behaving have a tendency to turn their displeasure into a judgment. Annoyed by their husbands' reluctance to help around the house, they might judge him to be lazy. Upset because the husband wants to stay home from church, they might judge him to be unspiritual.

Women who do that don't understand that they're falling prey to a very crafty scheme of the devil. They are actually prophesying those spirits into their home.

Truth be told, the devil uses all kinds of different schemes to undermine Christian marriages. He tells people, for instance, that just because they're Christians everything in their marriage will be perfect. It won't! All believers, and therefore all Christian marriages, are works in progress. So we have to be patient with each other.

A second lie the devil peddles, especially to naïve young women, is that they're automatically going to have a happy marriage just because they grew up in church and found there husband there. Sad to say, it doesn't work that way. Just because a man is in church doesn't mean he's right with God, or even that he's right for you.

What's more, God doesn't have grandchildren. Being raised in a Christian home and going to church all your life doesn't guarantee instant matrimonial harmony. Everyone has to have their own relationship with Jesus—and it's from that relationship that a good marriage will grow.

## *Do Something*

Every once in a while, I meet wives who are so overwhelmed by their situation they're like deer caught in headlights. They let the problems in their marriage paralyze them because they don't know what to do.

This is the advice I give those women: *do something.*

The lepers in Second Kings looked at one another and said, "Why sit here until we die?" They got up, faced their fears and lived! So if you're like they were and you're facing a seemingly hopeless situation, follow their example. Get up and take some steps in the right direction. Here are some tips to get you started:

1. Develop a quiet time and get to know Jesus through His Word.
2. Pray! Ask God for help.
3. Focus on getting your own emotional healing first.
4. If your husband refuses to go to a counselor, go alone.
5. Keep reminding yourself that he doesn't get it.
6. Find a group of women who will pray with you.
7. Fight for your marriage and your children.
8. Refuse to let the enemy isolate you.
9. Refuse to keep your situation a secret; talk about it.
10. Stop thinking that everything will be okay if you just give him more sex and keep the house clean. Yes, clean his house and give him sex, but don't think that will solve your problems.

11. Be honest, but also be kind and honor him.
12. Put your trust in God and understand that it's not up to you to change your husband; only God can change a heart.
13. Instead of staring at the mess in your marriage and feeling overwhelmed, remember: Nothing is impossible with God!

## *What's Love Got to Do with It?*

"But Karen," you might say, "I don't even love my husband anymore." So what? I spent *years* not loving Jimmy. Our marriage was an absolute model of hopelessness, pain, suffering, and dysfunction. But I can say with all honesty that when I look back over all the trauma and pain I went through, I wouldn't trade a moment of it because of what we have today.

I can also say that we wouldn't be where we are today if I'd set a time frame for Jimmy to change. When it comes to saving marriages, deadlines don't work. So if you have one, I'd advise you to forget about it.

As wives, we don't get to decide how long God is going to have to work on our husbands. Some men get it in two weeks. Some, like Jimmy, take five years. Some take 10 years and others take 20. Some harden their heart and never change.

"Well, if he might not change can't I cut my losses and get out?"

You can, I suppose. A lot of people do. But let me ask you something: Do you honestly believe you'll be a different person in a different marriage?

Trust me, you won't. If I'd never married Jimmy, it still would have taken me years of Holy Spirit surgery to get all that crud off of me and get me healed. The same principle will hold true for you. Married or not, you have to go to God and become whole if you're going to have a truly satisfying life. Bottom line, until you do that and forgive, you'll never be able to find what you want.

I've seen it proven out time and again, not only in my life but in the lives of others. When a woman's goal is to seek the Lord, she often ends up with a happy marriage. When her goal is a happy marriage, not so much.

Personally, I'll be forever glad I set my heart first and foremost on Jesus. He's the reason I can take my place on the set of MarriageToday and brave the glare of the television lights. He's the reason I have a story to tell. Jesus is the One who forgave me, saved me, redeemed me, and gave me a life better than anything I could have imagined…and He'll always be my first love.

Make no mistake about it, I love my husband, too—more than words can say. I love seeing his smile and hearing his voice. I love taking his hand seeing the joy in his eyes of just being with me. But every smile and tender word, every look of love I see in those eyes reminds me of Jesus…because without Him in my life and in my marriage I wouldn't have the incredible blessings I have today. I owe it all to Him!

# ABOUT THE AUTHOR

Karen Evans, along with her husband, Jimmy, founded the ministry of MarriageToday in 1994 as a way to bring help and healing to hurting couples. They co-host the television program, *MarriageToday*, which airs nationally to more than one hundred million households daily, and over 200 countries worldwide. Today, Jimmy and Karen speak at XO Conferences around the nation. You can also find more of their teachings on the XO Podcast Network and the XO Now streaming service. Jimmy and Karen have been married for 47 years, and they have two adult children and five grandchildren.